Grammar for Fiction Writers

A BUSY WRITER'S GUIDE

Marcy Kennedy & Chris Saylor

Tongue Untied Communications
ONTARIO, CANADA

Marcy Kennedy
marcykennedy@gmail.com
www.marcykennedy.com

Book Layout ©2013 BookDesignTemplates.com
Edited by Chris J. Saylor
Cover Design by Melinda VanLone

Grammar for Fiction Writers/ Marcy Kennedy —1st ed.
ISBN 978-0-9920371-8-5

Contents

Why a Grammar Guide for Fiction Writers?

'm in the odd category of people known as editors. Like writers, editors love words, but we also love the intricacies of grammar and punctuation that can make many writers feel like crying.

Because I know not everyone is like me, I wanted to create this book for people who struggle with grammar, as well as for those who might just want a refresher.

This book is specifically for fiction writers. The world of grammar is huge, but not everything applies to someone who's writing a novel or short story. In fact, some of the rules you were taught in your high school or college/university English class will actually hurt your fiction writing, not help it.

Like all the books in the Busy Writer's Guides series, *Grammar for Fiction Writers* is fluff-free. It won't teach you things you don't need to know. The focus is on teaching you the punctuation and grammar that are relevant to you as a fiction writer. While some elements are universally needed by writers (and are included), others are especially important for fiction writers (and have been given their own sections), and still others don't matter for fiction writers at

1

all (and, as such, aren't in this book). The goal of grammar for fiction writers is to make your writing clearer and more interesting for your readers.

This book was written with the goal of respecting your time—quickly and clearly teaching you what you need to know, in an approachable, friendly way, so that you can get back to writing your book. I know all these rules can be intimidating.

The point of this book isn't to turn you into a copy editor. If you decide to self-publish your book, you'll still need to hire a copy editor. None of us are objective enough to catch all our own errors.

When you finish, however, you should be able to write clean prose, not have your query letter or proposal rejected because of egregious errors, and pay less when you do hire a copy editor (the cleaner your book, the less a copy edit usually costs). You'll also be a more effective final pair of eyes for your book and catch anything that your copy editor or proofreader might have missed (because no one is perfect).

WHAT CAN YOU EXPECT IN THE REST OF THE BOOK?

Part One: Punctuation Basics

Chapter 1 – Possessives vs. Contractions

Chapter 2 – Comma Problems

Chapter 3 – Dashes, Semicolons, and Ellipses—Oh My!

Chapter 4 – How to Format Your Dialogue

Chapter 5 - Take It to the Page: Part One

Part Two: Knowing What Your Words Mean and What They Don't

Chapter 6 – Commonly Confused Words

HOW DO THE TAKE IT TO THE PAGE SECTIONS WORK?

If this is the first Busy Writer's Guide you've read, you're not familiar with what the Take It to the Page section is. If you have checked out a Busy Writer's Guide before, you're probably coming in with a set of expectations.

Before we dive into the meat of the book, we wanted to take the time to explain to you what a Take It to the Page section is and how the Take It to the Page sections in this book differ slightly from those in other books in the Busy Writer's Guide series.

The point of Busy Writer's Guides is to give you enough theory so that you can understand why things work and why they don't, enough examples to see how that theory looks in practice, and tips and exercises to help you take it to the pages of your own story with an editor's-eye view. The editing tips and exercises are usually placed in a Take It to the Page section that gives you a step-by-step guide you can follow when self-editing.

Because grammar is detail-oriented, many of the how-to suggestions you'd normally find in the Take It to the Page sections are going to come in the chapters themselves because they're largely memory tips for how to remember to do it right while you're writing. Beyond this, grammar is one of those places where there isn't a fast track to corrections. If you're fixing your book post-writing, you will need to read it through slowly and carefully.

But that doesn't mean this book is without any Take It to the Page sections. Wherever we can, we still want to give you tricks and shortcuts to make this grammar editing thing easier. And, as always, you can find a printable version of the Take It to the Page sections by using the link and password at the end of the first Take It to the Page section.

WHO ARE WE?

When it comes to buying a grammar book—especially a grammar book for fiction writers—it makes sense that you'd want to know who the authors are and whether or not they really know what they're talking about. So allow us to introduce ourselves.

Marcy Kennedy has been editing professionally since 2006, and she's worked on a variety of websites, articles, newsletters, brochures, essays, flysheets, grant proposals, and promotional materials. Her specialization, though, is in editing fiction. She's edited widely across genres, on novels, novellas, and short stories, and at all levels—from developmental editing to line editing to copy editing to proofreading.

Alongside her editing, Marcy is also an award-winning writer and teaches classes on the writing craft through W.A.N.A. International and at conferences. She's the author of the bestselling Busy Writer's Guides series of books.

Chris Saylor has been editing professionally since 2007. He's worked on a wide variety of documents, including short stories, novellas, pitch letters, book synopses, memoirs, dissertations, theses, essays, and web content. The clients he has done work for include the U.S. Department of Homeland Security, the Federal Bureau of Investigation, the U.S. Congress, the Jewish Federations of North America, Sharecare.com, Dove Press, *Molecular Vision*, Firefly Books, Ivey Publishing, Genpact, Hult Business School, Ted's Montana Grill, Scribendi.com, and Inkylo.com. He also does content writing and SEO optimization.

Chris is currently an in-house editor for Scribendi.com. He primarily works with nonfiction material, and thus takes a very technical approach to his editing and writing.

ONE MORE THING BEFORE WE START

Because this is a grammar book for fiction writers, we'll be using terms that we expect you, as a fiction writer, to already know. For example, we're assuming you know what point of view is or what a first-person narrator is. We won't be defining those terms within the body of the book. If you're not sure what those terms mean, we have included a quick glossary in Appendix C to help you out, and we recommend that you check out other books in the Busy Writer's Guide series, as well as Marcy's blog at www.marcykennedy.com.

PART ONE

Punctuation Basics

CHAPTER ONE

Throwdown: Possessives vs. Contractions

Just so we're all on the same page, I'm going to define possessives and contractions.

A *possessive* indicates that the object in question belongs to someone (or a group of someones). They possess it. A possessive is normally created by adding an apostrophe (') or an apostrophe plus *s* (*'s*) to the end of a word.

A *contraction* is a convention of the English language where we smash two words together to make them quicker and easier to say. We contract their length. We indicate that two words have been merged in this way by using an apostrophe.

Because both possessives and contractions use apostrophes, in some situations they can be easy to confuse.

I'm going to give you the basic rules for forming possessives first, and then I'll talk about the main causes of confusion.

RULES FOR FORMING A POSSESSIVE

If the word is singular, always add 's. It doesn't matter what letter ends the word.

> Chris's book
> Marcy's truck
> Paris's finest wine shop

But then, why are we sometimes told to leave off the *s* in words that already end in *s*, *x*, or *z*?

If it would sound awkward to have the additional *s* sound, it's acceptable to omit the *s*. However, it's always correct to include it, so when in doubt, include the *s*.

> Mrs. Williams's dog escaped.
> Mrs. Williams' dog escaped.

And for a few words, common usage has created anomalies.

> Achilles' heel
> Euripides' plays
> Brahms' lullaby
> For goodness' sake

If you think something is the exception to the rule, the easiest way to check is to look it up in the dictionary.

If the word is plural and already ends in *s*, just add an apostrophe.

> Both dogs' noses were wet.

> The Joneses' apartment was barely big enough for two.

If the word is plural and doesn't end in an *s*, add the apostrophe plus an *s*.

> The children's desks needed to be replaced before school could continue.

> The women's fashion show was canceled because of the weather.

WHERE THE PROBLEMS START

The exception to the rule of adding an apostrophe (with or without an *s*) to form a possessive is with personal pronouns.

The most problematic combinations are *your/you're, its/it's,* and *their/they're/there.*

In all these cases, if it includes an apostrophe, it's a contraction of two words. The apostrophe shows you that two words have been joined. Think of it like the grammatical version of a wedding ring.

> *You're = you are*
> You're giving me a headache with all this grammar talk.
> *They're = they are*
> They're going to buy a new dictionary.
> *It's = it is/it has*
> It's stupid that the English language uses apostrophes for both possessives and contractions.

Even though other possessives are formed using an apostrophe, possessives involving *you, they,* and *it* aren't, because if they were, there would be no way to distinguish them from contractions involving the same words.

The possessives of these words form in their own rebellious way.

> *You're = you + are*
> *Your* = possessive, as in "I love your book."

They're = they + are

Their = possessive, as in "Their house is blue."

And for fun, English also gives us...

There = a place ("I've been there") or a pronoun ("There is no way I'm jumping off that cliff.")

It's = it + is

Its = possessive

Here's a little trick for keeping these straight. (If memory tricks don't work for you, don't worry, but I like to give them for the people who do find that they help.)

Think of the apostrophe in contractions as a <u>wedding ring</u> between two words when it comes to <u>personal</u> pronouns. In a marriage, two <u>persons</u> become "one," and they should never consider each other a <u>possession</u>.

CHAPTER TWO

Comma Problems

Commas are, understandably, the biggest bugaboo for writers. Not only are some situations of comma placement personal preference rather than hard rule, but different style guides also set out different rules.

Yet commas are also extremely important, since their placement can change the meaning of a sentence, as well as keep you from saying something unintentionally ridiculous.

Let's look at an example to show you what I mean.

> Betty insisted Edgar planned the bank robbery.

> Betty, insisted Edgar, planned the bank robbery.

In the first sentence, Betty is saying Edgar was the mastermind. In the second sentence, Edgar is saying Betty was the mastermind.

Despite their fluidity, commas do come with some firm rules. In this chapter, I'm going to focus on the ones that matter most to us as fiction writers. If you get them correct, most people won't notice that the others are missing. Your editor can then fix the other nitpicky comma areas in your book.

COMMA SPLICES MUST DIE

A comma splice is when you use a comma to connect independent clauses (clauses that could stand alone as complete sentences) without using a conjunction (a word like *and*, *but*, or *or*). You're splicing two full sentences together.

> I don't know what I was thinking, I shouldn't have gone there.

You can fix a comma splice in three ways.

> *Add a conjunction:* I don't know what I was thinking, but I shouldn't have gone there.
> *Replace the comma with a period:* I don't know what I was thinking. I shouldn't have gone there.
> *Replace the comma with a semicolon:* I don't know what I was thinking; I shouldn't have gone there.

Unless you're writing for academia, I recommend not using a semicolon. We'll take about semicolons more in the next chapter.

You'll hear some authors claim that they're using a comma splice because they want to create a sense that their character is rushing their words. Don't do this. It doesn't do what they want it to. It only makes them look like they don't know how to use periods and commas properly. And it opens you up to complaints from readers who think you need a better edit or proofread of your book.

DO <u>NOT</u> SPLIT THE SUBJECT AND PREDICATE WITH A COMMA

This is true even if you're using a compound subject.
But you might ask, "Don't split the what?"

Every complete sentence needs two things: a *subject* and a *predicate.*

The **subject** is the thing the sentence is about. (Think "test subject" in an experiment.)

> *I* walked to the store.
> *The brown puppy* is cute.
> *Emily and Bob* own the house.
> *Whales* swim.

The **predicate** tells us something about the subject. It might tell us what the subject did, what it looks like, etc. (I like to remember this as a friend of *prediction*, which tells us something about the future.)

> I *walked to the store.*
> The brown puppy *is cute.*
> Emily and Bob *own the house.*
> Whales *swim.*

The important thing to remember about the predicate is that it contains a verb. (A verb describes an action, state of being, or relationship between two things.) *Walked, is, own,* and *swim* in the examples above are all verbs.

So, when I say not to split the subject and the predicate with a comma, this is what I'm telling you <u>not</u> to do.

> The dog and the cat, were the best of friends despite their different species.

In this example, you shouldn't use a comma. The dog and the cat are both the subject of the sentence, and the comma cuts them off from the verb (*were*) in the predicate.

USE COMMAS AROUND NON-RESTRICTIVE CLAUSES, INCLUDING THOSE THAT START WITH "WHICH"

A *non-restrictive clause* is one the sentence doesn't need to make sense. It merely provides additional information about a subject that's already been clearly identified.

A *restrictive clause* is one the sentence needs. Without it, the sentence won't make sense or won't say the same thing. It restricts the meaning in some way.

I'll give you two examples of non-restrictive clauses.

> The door, which looked to be 100 years old, squeaked when we opened it.

> My cats, both declawed as kittens, still think they have claws and try to scratch the furniture.

To put this another way, if you can take out those extra words in the middle and the sentence still says what you meant it to, you need to set those extra words off with commas.

(Don't worry about the definition of a clause right now. We'll get to that later.)

Related to using commas around non-restrictive clauses is another rule...

When your independent clause is preceded by a dependent clause or a phrase, separate them with a comma.

We'll talk about independent and dependent clauses more in Chapter 19. For now, just remember that an independent clause could exist as a full sentence without anything else and a dependent clause couldn't.

Take a look at these two examples. I've bolded the independent clause and left the dependent clause plain.

Whenever you're ready to go, **I'll start the car**.

According to the weather forecast, **we'll be getting snow today**.

WHAT ABOUT SERIAL COMMAS?

A serial comma involves placing a comma after every item in a series: "I love eating jelly beans, chocolate, and cranberries."

You could write this without the serial comma: "I love eating jelly beans, chocolate and cranberries."

Serial commas aren't mandatory, but they are recommended by most major style guides for a very simple reason—they eliminate the risk of being unintentionally funny or unintentionally unclear.

A housewife's job involves more than cleaning, cooking and birthing babies.

Is it just me, or does that sound like she's serving up roast baby for dinner? But add a serial comma and we have...

A housewife's job involves more than cleaning, cooking, and birthing babies.

Now we have a clear tribute to mothers rather than cannibalism.

The only thing worse than being boring is being unintentionally funny. Once people laugh *at* you, that's all they're going to remember about you. They at least forget about you if you're boring.

I live by the *better safe than sorry* rule. If I always use a serial comma, I never run the risk of leaving it out when I should have put it in. The only time you should leave serial commas out is if your publisher specifically requests that you do so or the style guide you're working with specifically says to avoid them.

CHAPTER THREE

Dashes, Semicolons, and Ellipses—Oh My!

D ashes, semicolons, and ellipses also serve as road signs for readers. They aren't used nearly as often as commas, but it's just as important to get these right as it is to get commas right—if not more so. In this chapter, we're going to look at how fiction writers can use these different forms of punctuation to make sure their meaning is clear.

DASHES

There are three types of dashes you need to know: hyphens, en dashes, and em dashes.

Hyphens

Dashes are most commonly used in writing to denote compound adjectives—that is, when you have two or more words working together to modify the same word or phrase. In these cases, dashes are known as hyphens. They aren't always strictly necessary, but they do make things a little clearer.

I'll give you a couple examples so you can see this in action.

> **Wrong:** Jennifer is soft spoken.
>
> **Right:** Jennifer is soft-spoken.

Soft-spoken is modifying *Jennifer,* so there's a simple way to check if you should use a hyphen or not.

Remember, when we say one word modifies another, we're meaning that it indicates or describes the place (e.g., *above*), the time (e.g., *later*), the manner (e.g., *loudly*), the circumstance (e.g., *accidentally*), or the degree (e.g., *really*) of the word it's connected to.

So what type of woman is Jennifer? She's a soft-spoken one. Can we break up *soft* and *spoken* without either losing or changing the meaning?

If we were to say *Jennifer is soft*, it wouldn't mean the same thing.

We also wouldn't say *Jennifer is spoken.* That doesn't make any sense.

Because we can't separate those two words, they need to be hyphenated.

I'll show you a case where we could separate them.

> Jane has dark, curly hair.

We don't hyphenate *dark* and *curly.*

> Jane has dark hair.
> Jane has curly hair.

Both work.

Let's look at another example where we do need a hyphen.

> **Wrong:** The Broncos play in a mile high stadium.

Right: The Broncos play in a mile-high stadium.

Apply our little test again.

The Broncos play in a mile stadium...Nope.

The Broncos play in a high stadium...Maybe, but it wouldn't mean the same thing.

But remember that, as problematic as it is to leave hyphens out when you need them, you also don't want to add them in where they don't belong.

Wrong: The game I bought cost twenty-dollars.

Right: The game I bought cost twenty dollars.

In this case, you don't hyphenate *twenty* and *dollars* because they're not modifying the same word. Instead, *twenty* modifies *dollars*.

How many dollars? Twenty dollars.

En Dashes

En dashes are most commonly used to denote ranges or relationships.

1999–2002 (range)
Mother–daughter conflict (relationship)

In Microsoft Word for Windows, the keyboard shortcut for an en dash is CTRL + minus sign.

Em Dashes

Em dashes are used to insert parenthetical expressions. You can tell a parenthetical expression because you can take it out of the sentence and the sentence still makes sense. But the parenthetical expression doesn't make sense apart from the rest of the sentence. You can think about it almost like a parasite (*para*site, *pare*nthetical). It needs the sentence to survive, but the sentence doesn't need it.

> This part of the sentence makes sense—though this part doesn't—so I inserted a pair of em dashes.

I'll give you another example, one that you might see in a novel.

> John loved her look—her shoes, her hair, her dress, even her artfully done makeup—and thanked Fate yet again that she had chosen to marry him, plain as he was.

Em dashes are also used when a character's dialogue (including internal dialogue) is interrupted by something else. This use for an em dash is covered in more detail in Chapter Four.

In Microsoft Word for Windows, the keyboard shortcut for an em dash is CTRL + ALT + minus sign.

SEMICOLONS

Semicolons are used when you want to join two related sentences together into a single sentence. A good way to determine when to use semicolons is if two related sentences make grammatical sense on their own.

> I love pizza. Pepperoni is my favorite.

Or...

> I love pizza; pepperoni is my favorite.

Both versions are correct. That said, there's a running joke in the fiction world that you only get one semicolon per career, so you need to use it wisely. While that might be a little extreme, the point behind the joke is true. In fiction, we should avoid using semicolons whenever possible. If there's a way to write the sentence without one, we should choose the option that avoids the semicolon.

I know that might sound arbitrary at first, but the reasons behind it are valid. Semicolons can look pretentious or awkward because many people don't understand what they mean or how to use them correctly.

Worse, though, is that semicolons often look downright stupid or out of place. The worst offender is when we use a semicolon in our dialogue. No one speaks with semicolons.

Try it. I bet you can speak in such a way to imply a comma, a period, an em dash, or an ellipses. And I bet you can't speak in such a way as to make it clear that you're speaking a semicolon rather than a period.

When we're writing fiction, the one time we do need to use semicolons is in a complex sentence where commas alone wouldn't provide enough clarity. The semicolons take the place of the serial commas that would usually separate the main elements in the sentence.

Let me give you an example (since this is one of those times where it's definitely easier to understand once you see it).

> When Anna thought of summer at the beach, she always thought of the sunshine; *the sand, water, and crisp ocean air*; and the fresh seafood.

The bolded part is the part that makes us need semi-colons. That sub-section of the sentence needs commas, and so we need something else to separate it off from the other sub-sections. Look at a similar, simplified version where we wouldn't need the semicolons.

> When Anna thought of summer at the beach, she always thought of the sunshine, *the ocean air*, and the fresh seafood.

See how the bolded part doesn't have commas anymore?

ELLIPSES

Ellipses are used in two main ways. Nonfiction writers will use them primarily when quoting a person or piece of writing to indicate the omission of a portion of the quoted material.

As fiction writers, we use them in a different way. Ellipses show a character's words trailing off in either their spoken or internal dialogue. The character might be unable to bear finishing the thought or speaking the words, or they might be trailing off to allow a question or accusation to hang in the air.

Let's say our point-of-view character has just received the news that she's developed lung cancer after having beat breast cancer less than a year before. Her reaction to the news might go something like this...

> She slumped forward, her face buried in her hands. After she'd battled so hard to... She shook her head. "It wasn't supposed to be like this."

Before we move on, we'll look at one more instance where a character might use ellipses in spoken dialogue. In this example, we have a mother and a daughter. The daughter has been pestering her mother to allow her to get her driver's license. Up to this point, the mother has refused. Now, an eighteen-year-old boy has shown up at the door to drive her daughter to school.

> "I don't see what the big deal is," Lara said. "You won't let me get my license and I hate riding the bus so..." She shrugged, grabbed her backpack, and headed for the door. "Besides, it's just a ride. It's not like we're dating."

CHAPTER FOUR

How to Format Dialogue

This chapter is an excerpt from *How to Write Dialogue: A Busy Writer's Guide*. For those of you who've already read *How to Write Dialogue*, this will be a refresher, but properly formatting dialogue is tricky enough and important enough that I felt it was essential to include it in *Grammar for Fiction Writers* as well.

The quickest way to make your work look more professional is to format your dialogue properly. This is the foundation for everything else you'll learn about dialogue. (If you're interested in learning more about dialogue, pick up a copy of *How to Write Dialogue: A Busy Writer's Guide*.) Once you learn these formatting requirements, you'll do them naturally as you write and won't have to think about them.

ONE SPEAKER PER PARAGRAPH

Every time you have a new speaker, you need a new paragraph, even if the dialogue is only one word long.

Whether you personally like the look of it, this is what readers expect. It makes your dialogue easier to understand because they're able to quickly recognize a change in speaker even before you identify who's talking. It also helps you limit the use of speaker attributions (more on that later).

Wrong:

"Ella? Are you here?" Sarah asked. Ella popped up from behind the desk, cobwebs in her hair and a dirty cloth dangling from her fingers. "I just need another ten minutes to finish."

Right:

"Ella? Are you here?" Sarah asked.

Ella popped up from behind the desk, cobwebs in her hair and a dirty cloth dangling from her fingers. "I just need another ten minutes to finish."

CHOOSE THE CORRECT FORM OF PUNCTUATION

Improper punctuation of dialogue is one of the most common mistakes I see in manuscripts I edit and critique.

Use a comma at the end of a segment of dialogue (even a complete sentence) when followed by a tag.

A **tag** is a word such as *said* or *asked*.

"I hate cinnamon jelly beans," Marcy said.

Use a question mark without a comma for a question.

This applies to exclamation marks, too.

"Do you like cinnamon jelly beans?" Marcy asked.

I could have replaced *asked* with *said* here and the punctuation would remain the same.

> Extra Tip: Although it might look strange at first, you can use the tag *said* even if your speaker is asking a question. The question mark alone indicates a question, and technically we're speaking whether the words come out as a question, an exclamation, or a shout.
> *"Do you like cinnamon jelly beans?" Marcy said.*
> This is an option you have, not a requirement.

If a tag is dividing a sentence, use a comma at the end of the first section of dialogue (even if the comma wouldn't normally go there in the same sentence if it wasn't dialogue) and use a comma after the tag.

"I hate cinnamon jelly beans," Marcy said, "because they burn my tongue."

Use a period after a tag when the first segment of dialogue is a complete sentence. Use a comma at the end of the dialogue preceding the tag.

"I hate cinnamon jelly beans," Marcy said. "I refuse to eat them."

Use a dash when dialogue is cut off or interrupted.

Do not add any other punctuation.

"It wasn't my—"
"Enough excuses."

Remember to use an ellipsis for dialogue that fades away.

"I just…" She wrapped her arms around her stomach. "I thought he loved me."

Use exclamation marks sparingly!

Sometimes you need an exclamation point to add emotional context, but they're usually a sign that you're trying to bolster weak dialogue. They're also distracting!! And if you use them too often, they lose their emphasis!!

Don't use colons or semicolons in your dialogue at all.

While this might seem like an arbitrary rule, colons and semicolons just look unnatural in dialogue. For the most part, you should avoid them in your fiction entirely.

Punctuation almost always goes inside the quotation marks in North America.

If you're not in North America, check some of the traditionally published books on your shelf to see where they place punctuation.

CHAPTER FIVE

Take It to the Page: Part One

Many of the Take It to the Page sections use the Find feature of your word processing program to make things quicker for you. This feature will become one of your best editing friends.

If you have a word processing program (like Microsoft Word 2010 or newer) that will highlight every instance of a word that you search for, your task will be easier, but you can also do this in programs that give you the results one by one.

Step 1

In the Find box, enter a semicolon. Check each instance. Can it be replaced by a period? If so, swap it out.

Step 2

Use the Find feature to search for ellipses. Make sure you check for both ... (three periods together) and . . . (three periods each separated by a space). Does each ellipses represent either speech or internal dialogue trailing off? If not, replace it with the correct punctuation. For example, you might have accidentally used ellipses to signal dialogue that was interrupted, but the correct punctuation in that case is a dash.

Step 3

Search for the following. The first two examples have no space between the punctuation and the quotation mark. Make sure to include a space between the punctuation and the quotation marks in the second two examples.

,"
."
, "
. "

(In case you find that difficult to read, it's comma-quotation mark, period-quotation mark, comma-space-quotation mark, and period-space-quotation mark.)

Check that you've used them correctly. This won't catch everything, but it will clean up your dialogue punctuation significantly.

Step 4

Search for exclamation marks. Read out loud each passage of dialogue with an exclamation mark to see if you actually would (and can) exclaim the passage. Does the sentence need it to make the meaning clear? Can you rewrite the sentence to make it more powerful so that it doesn't need the exclamation mark?

If you'd like a printable version of the complete revision checklist (material from all the Take It to the Page chapters), go to www.marcykennedy.com/grammar and use the password below.

Password: commasplice

PART TWO

Knowing What Your Words Mean and What They Don't

Commonly Confused Words

Words that are pronounced the same way (even though they have different spellings) or that are spelled exactly the same way but can have two different meanings are known as *homophones*.

I know. Homophones make it seem like the first English speakers were being cruel in the way they developed the language.

I'm going to go through some of the most common problem pairs (and trios!) for you, along with some tricks to help you keep them straight.

I'm also going to provide you with a little editor's secret at the end.

TO/TOO/TWO

Not only do these all sound the same, but they're only one letter different from each other.

***Two* is a <u>number</u>.**

> Example: If you already have one chocolate bar and I give you mine, then you have *two* chocolate bars and I'm going to be asking you to share.

<u>Memory Trick</u>: Hold up two fingers. They form half a W. *To* and *too* don't have that shape in them. They are not numbers. If that doesn't work for you, remember that *two* (as a number) starts the same way as *twins*.

***Too* is an adverb expressing the idea of "excessively," "also," or "as well."**

> Example: This word has one too many *o*'s in it.

<u>Memory Trick</u>: And that's the trick to remembering it. It has an excessive number of *o*'s.

***To* is a preposition. It's used to begin a prepositional phrase or an infinitive.**

The best way to remember *to* is to place it where neither *two* nor *too* will work.

> Example 1: I went to church on Sunday. (preposition)
> Example 2: I want to eat your chocolate. (infinitive)

(And no, you don't need to worry about what adverbs, prepositions, or infinitives are for the most part. Writing isn't like an English class where you're going to need to diagram a sentence. As we go along, we'll tell you the parts you need to remember.)

OTHER NOT-SO-FUN COMBOS

Tick/Tic

A *tick* is a small creature you want to pick off as quickly as possible. (See how *pick* and *tick* are only one letter different?) A *tic* is a muscle spasm or unconscious action.

Reign/Rein

Reign is what a sovereign does. *Reins* are what you use to control a horse when you're riding.

The king wants a long reign (the longer word). You want to keep a tight rein on a rebellious horse (the shorter word) so it doesn't run away with you.

Principle/Principal

These both have various definitions, so my recommendation is that you turn to your dictionary if you're not 100% sure which to use.

Principle is most commonly used to refer to the standards by which a person acts.

> His **principles** wouldn't allow him to shoot an unarmed man.

Principal most commonly refers to the administrator who runs a school.

Remember that the one with *pal* in it usually refers to a person. You can't be pals with a standard.

Desert/Dessert

Dessert has two *s*'s. You want more of a *dessert* (because it's good to eat) than you would of a *desert* (where you might die of thirst).

Affect/Effect

These two are annoying because of the nuances involved. I'm going to give you a general guideline that's going to allow you to get it right 99.9% of the time.

Affect is generally used as a verb (an action word) meaning "to influence."

> The icy roads **affected** the way I drove yesterday.

I could just as easily have written "The icy roads **influenced** the way I drove yesterday."

Effect is generally used as a noun meaning "a result."

> The **effect** of the sleepless night on her mood was startling.

I could have written this as "The **result** of her sleepless night on her mood was startling."

Grammar Girl has a helpful little mnemonic for this one that I'm going to borrow because I haven't heard or been able to come up with a better one.

> The <u>a</u>rrow <u>a</u>ffected the <u>a</u>ardvark. (*The arrow influenced the aardvark* makes sense. *The arrow resulted the aardvark* doesn't. Therefore, affect = influence.)

> The <u>e</u>ffect was <u>e</u>ye-popping. (*The result was eye-popping* makes sense. *The influence was eye-popping* doesn't. Therefore, effect = result.)

Lose/Loose

Lose is what happens when you're not the winner or when you can't find something. *Loose* is another way of saying that something is freed from its restraints or not bound in any way.

Loose has two *o*'s. If you lose one, you get...*lose*.

Bear/Bare

A *bear* is an animal. *Bare* is what you are when you're naked.

Naked = bare. The vowels are in the same order.

Where/Wear/Were

Wear is what you do with your clothes so that you're not naked. *Where* refers to a place, a location, or a source.

Here's the quick way to remember the difference.

W<u>here</u> are you going? I'm going <u>here</u>.

Were gets confused with the others because it looks like it should be pronounced the same way but it isn't. *Were* is the plural form of *was*. You **don't** pronounce it like **were**wolf. You pronounce it as *whir*.

As long as you remember how *were* is pronounced, you won't confuse it with *wear* and *where*. To do this, you can use a silly little mnemonic:

Were you bitten by a werewolf?

When you say that sentence aloud, you won't be tempted to pronounce it incorrectly.

THE EDITOR'S SECRET

I could go on like this for pages, but...

Here's the dirty little editor's secret I promised.

Even editors can't keep the meanings of all the confusable words in the English language straight. We don't need to, and neither do you.

You just have to know when you're using a word that's easily confused with another and then look it up.

I recommend that writers buy a copy of *The Dictionary of Confusable Words* and spend a little time flipping through it. (You'll find a lot of options when you search for this on Amazon. It doesn't really matter which one you get.) Try to familiarize yourself with the words that can be easily confused. To get you started, we've also included a list of 200 sets of commonly confused words.

CHAPTER SEVEN

Imaginary Words and Phrases

At first, this chapter might seem similar to the chapter on words that are misused. But here's the difference: This lesson covers words and phrases that don't actually exist or that mean the opposite of what we're trying to say. We use them, thinking they're real, but we're actually just hitting on a mutation of the real thing.

COULD OF, SHOULD OF, WOULD OF

"I could of finished that ten-ounce steak if I wanted to, but I'm watching my waistline."

This mistake crops up when people write the same way they speak. When we speak, we often slur *could've* (the contraction of *could have*) so that it sounds like *could of.*

Of can be used correctly in many different ways, but this isn't one of them. You might be able to get away with it in speech (and in your dialogue), but not in the rest of your writing.

IRREGARDLESS

Irregardless isn't a real word. People who say this usually mean *regardless*.

Regardless means "showing or having no regard for something, in spite of or without concern for the advice given." When you act regardless of something, you're ignoring that thing.

> "You might think that way is best. Regardless, I'm going to do it my way."

> He acted regardless of the consequences.

I COULD CARE LESS

Some people will try to argue that this is a regional thing. But it isn't a regional thing—it's an I-don't-understand-that-what-I'm-saying-is-the-opposite-of-what-I-actually-mean thing.

I couldn't care less = There is no situation in which I could have less concern for, care for, or interest in whatever I was just talking about.

> I couldn't care less whether he lives or dies. He's a jerk.

> I couldn't care less if you throw that out. I never liked it anyway.

I could care less = I still care a little because I could care a little less than I currently do.

No one says "I could care less" and means what it actually means. What they really mean to say is "I couldn't care less."

FOR ALL INTENSIVE PURPOSES

Intensive means "extreme" or "very great" or "to a high degree."

For all intensive purposes, the watch was broken.

Does that mean the watch doesn't work when you mountain climb or deep sea dive, but it works fine if you want to check the time when you're at work?

Unless you're meaning that the situation you're talking about is intense (in other words, extreme), what you mean to write is ***for all intents and purposes***.

For all intents and purposes means "in every practical sense" or "in every practical way."

SUPPOSABLY

Yeah...that's not a word.

Supposedly means "to assume or accept something as true when there are no facts to support it."

Supposedly she cheated on her husband, but neither
of them are willing to talk about what happened.

Supposably is another example that we should be careful about trying to spell the way we speak.

CHAPTER EIGHT

Crutch Words

This chapter is a short one about three crutch words that you want to avoid.

LITERALLY

Literally is often used to add hyperbole to a sentence. (Hyperbole is an intentional exaggeration.) But because *literally* in the strictest sense means that something took place, it can make for some humorous sentences.

"My head literally exploded."

Ouch! Glad I'm not the one who has to clean that up.

"I walked a hundred miles to get there. Literally."

I bet you have some nasty blisters on your feet.

Unless you're intentionally using literally in character dialogue, this word doesn't belong in your fiction. You don't need to tell the reader that something actually happened in the strictest sense. If you describe it as happening in your story world, they will know that it literally happened.

The one exception to this would be if you're writing a first person narrator, but even then, use *literally* with caution.

OBVIOUSLY

Obviously should only be used to describe an action that is easily observable, recognized, or understood. Not everyone uses it that way.

> "Obviously, he shouldn't have bought that car. Everyone knows they're lemons."

It probably wasn't obvious at the time that he shouldn't have purchased the car. If it was obvious, he wouldn't have done it.

Just like *literally*, this should only be used strategically in dialogue (or with a first person narrator) and never in the prose of your fiction.

HONESTLY

Honestly often gets used to try to add veracity to a statement. Unfortunately, it implies that you otherwise would have lied.

> "I honestly don't know why she did that."

It makes you sound like you're trying too hard to be believed. If you're adding this to dialogue and that's the impression you're trying to give, go ahead. Otherwise, you're best to avoid *honestly*, too.

Because these terms are so often used incorrectly in speech, it can be difficult to strip them from our writing, but it's worth trying our best.

CHAPTER NINE

Weak Words

Weak words are words that don't pull their own weight in a sentence. Most of the time, they're useless. So useless, in fact, that, by taking them out, you make the sentence stronger.

At first this might seem like a strange chapter to include in a grammar book. Technically speaking, there's nothing wrong with weak words. But this is a book on grammar for fiction writers, and so one of the things we have to look at in terms of grammar is tightening up our writing and bringing it to life by removing useless words from our sentences.

In this chapter, I'm going to break weak words down into three categories:

Weasel words that you should try to remove whenever possible.

Helping and state-of-being verbs that you should try to replace with stronger verbs.

Unspecific words that you should try to replace with more specific words.

WEASEL WORDS

Weasel words are the easiest to deal with because, 90 percent of the time, we can simply remove them from the sentence and all will be well. Even when you can't remove them, though, they're a sign of weak or generic writing, and we should try to find a way to rework the sentence.

Let me give you a couple examples.

The night was ***very*** cold.

You could simply take the *very* out.

The night was cold.

But one could argue that there's a difference between *cold* and *very cold*. This is a good example of how weasel words lead to generic writing. By removing them, we're forced to find a more descriptive way to show (rather than tell) what we're writing about.

The night air bit her skin and froze her breath the instant it left her lips.

That says *very cold*, but it does it in a stronger way because it allows the reader to feel it by bringing back memories of times they've felt this degree of cold.

Other weasel words to search for include *almost, approximately, began, big, down, important, just, many, nearly, pretty, quite, really, started, that, very,* and *well.*

The one thing you want to watch out for is that you don't delete any of these words without looking at them in context first.

For example, there's a difference between a character who says...

"I'm ready to go."

And a character who says...

"I'm almost ready to go."

HELPING AND STATE-OF-BEING VERBS

Helping verbs include *may, might, must, be, being, been, am, are, is, was, were, do, does, did, should, could, would, have, had, has, will, can,* and *shall*.

State-of-being verbs include *is, am, were, was, are, be, being,* and *been*.

We want to avoid these verbs as much as possible in favor of stronger, more active verbs, but we also want to avoid them because they can indicate telling rather than showing.

One of the most common mistakes I see in the work of newer writers looks like this...

He ***was walking*** down the street.

They do it because they want to give the impression of an ongoing activity, but in fiction, it's unnecessary. Instead you'd want to write it this way...

He ***walked*** down the street.

By removing the *was* verb and replacing it with the stronger *walked*, you've described the same thing for the reader, but you've done it in a tighter, more active way. The best part is that it's usually a simple fix in these cases to remove the weak verb.

Helping and state-of-being verbs require more work to fix when they're used to tell rather than show something. I can't go in-depth into showing vs. telling in this book (if you want more on that, check out my book *Mastering Showing and Telling in Your Fiction*), but let me give you an example so you can see how helping or state-of-being verbs can be a red flag that you might be telling rather than showing.

> Telling: She **was** ugly.

In this example, we're telling the reader that she's ugly, but they don't know *what* about her makes her ugly. *Ugly* is a subjective term. What's ugly to one person won't be ugly to another. There are also different degrees of ugly. When we tell the reader that a character is ugly, we don't give them anything to picture in their minds. Here's one way we could show this instead.

> Showing: Richard couldn't stop himself from staring at the button-sized wart in the middle of her forehead. Even if she didn't want it removed, couldn't she have at least plucked the hair?

One or two carefully selected details will dynamically show us that a person is old or ugly, cruel or a flirt. Moreover, showing also gives us insight into the point-of-view (POV) character. What our characters notice and how they choose to describe it says a lot about them. Richard finds the woman's wart ugly. Another character might not have even noticed it.

UNSPECIFIC WORDS

Both weasel words and helping and state-of-being verbs could have been included under unspecific words because of how they tend to tell rather than show, but I broke them up because of the slight differences between them. In this section, I want to focus on words that are weak specifically because of how vague and generic they are.

Got/Get

Get (and its forms) isn't always wrong, but you want to be careful because it can lead to confusion. It means "to receive," "to take possession," or "to obtain." However, some people also use it in place of *have*.

Let me show you how this becomes a problem.

> I **got** five dollars.

Does this mean "I have five dollars," as in "I currently possess five dollars"? Or does it mean "someone gave me five dollars"?

To avoid vagueness like this, you should rewrite your sentence.

> Grandpa gave me five dollars.
> I have only five dollars to my name right now.

As you go through your writing, don't assume that your *got* sentences are clear. Make sure they are.

Things

Like *got*, *things* isn't wrong, but we often use it as the lazy way to escape putting in the work to define what we mean by *things*. *Things* could stand in for *problems* or *reasons*, which are two very different things.

When your character says, "I have things to do," what does she mean? Does she mean she has errands to run? A house to clean? A doctor's appointment? The only time you should have a character saying they have "things to do" is if they're being intentionally vague, such as if they don't want their girlfriend to know that they're planning a surprise proposal. But even then, why not have them give a more specific excuse?

Moved/Took/Looked

How many times have you written something like this?

He *moved* across the room.

Grammatically, there's nothing wrong with this sentence. The problem comes from its vagueness. It doesn't give the reader a clear picture of the way your character is moving.

Look at these three possible types of movement.

He *shuffled* across the room.
He *stalked* across the room.
He *sauntered* across the room.

In each sentence, we have him moving across the room, but they're extremely different types of movement. Don't leave your reader guessing.

Both *took* and *looked* fall into the same category as moved.

She *took* the letter from him.

This doesn't show us what's happening.

She *snatched* the letter from him.

She *delicately plucked* the letter from him using only her thumb and forefinger, as if she were afraid contact with it would contaminate her.

Two different emotions are behind those ways of taking the letter.

Here's the one I see most often in my editing work.

She *looked* at him.

But *how* did she look at him? Was it a furtive glance from the corner of her eyes as if she didn't want to be caught? Was she glaring? Was she giving him an I-dare-you-to-try-it look?

None of these unspecific words are technically wrong, but you're shortchanging your reader and yourself.

CHAPTER TEN

Connotation vs. Denotation

As we said in the introduction, this is a book on grammar for fiction writers. That means we're delving into areas where you aren't wrong for using a specific word, but that doesn't mean you're right, either. You saw this in the previous chapter on weak words, where a word technically worked in a sentence, but it wasn't as strong and clear as it could be. In this chapter, we're going to look at the connotation vs. the denotation of a word.

Denotation refers to the dictionary definition of a word. This is its literal meaning.

The *connotation* of a word, though, refers to the emotional baggage the word carries, the associations we, as a society, formed around it. As fiction writers, one of the tricks we can use to add layers of meaning to our work is to consider the connotations of the words we use.

I'll give you an example. Here are the denotations of two words, compliments of the dictionary.

Thin: having little flesh, spare, lean
Skinny: very lean or thin

Denotatively, they mean the same thing.

Connotatively, they don't.

When we say someone is thin, we usually mean it in a positive way. The connotation attached to *thin* is that thin is healthy and the opposite of fat. When we say someone is skinny, it carries the connotation of unhealthy, an eating disorder, or starvation.

So when you're having your point-of-view character describe someone they've just met, someone who is lean, you need to consider what you want to imply. Do you want to imply that the lean character is fit, perhaps a runner? Or do you want to imply that this character has a secret—a spouse who's starving them, not enough money to buy groceries, or maybe anorexia?

Let's take another example.

Naked: being without clothing or covering
Nude: naked or unclothed

Same denotation. Different connotation.

You wouldn't say that someone was part of a naked colony or that it's a naked beach. We talk about nudist colonies and nude beaches.

Naked carries with it the connotation of shame and inappropriateness. You're naked if you're not wearing clothing when you should be.

You're nude if you're not wearing clothing in the appropriate setting. A nude model. A nude beach.

A woman is nude with the husband she loves but naked when she's raped by a stranger. You would only describe a woman as *naked* in front of her husband if you want to suggest that she's ashamed of the way her body looks, or if he's abusive. Being aware of the connotation allows you to add that subtext that enriches a story.

Denotation vs. connotation isn't something to sweat over during your first draft. It's something you'll want to watch for as you go through on your polishing edit.

CHAPTER ELEVEN

Take It to the Page: Part Two

Hint for Part Two: If you're writing in present tense rather than in past tense, make sure you adjust any searches you do to reflect that. For example, if you're writing in past tense, you'd search for *looked*. If you're writing in present tense, you'd search for *looks*.

Step 1

When it comes to homophones (words that sound alike but are spelled differently), you probably have some that you have no problem with and some that always trip you up. A good trick to speed up the editing process is to keep a list of the ones you commonly stumble over. Use the Find feature of your word processing program to search for these pairs and make sure you've used them correctly. If you're just starting out and don't have a list of your own yet, to get you started, we've included a list in Appendix B of some of the most commonly confused words.

Step 2

Do a search for the following words/phrases. If you've used them outside of spoken dialogue, make sure you correct them. If you've used them within spoken dialogue, make sure you've done it for a reason.

- ✓ Could of
- ✓ Should of
- ✓ Would of
- ✓ Irregardless
- ✓ I could care less
- ✓ For all intensive purposes
- ✓ Supposably

Step 3

Do a search for the following words. Have you used them purposefully and strategically? If not, rewrite the sentence to remove them.

- ✓ honestly
- ✓ literally
- ✓ obviously

Step 4

Use the Find feature to search for the following weasel words. Does your sentence need them to make sense? If not, delete them.

- ✓ a bit
- ✓ a little
- ✓ about

- ✓ actually
- ✓ again
- ✓ all
- ✓ almost
- ✓ already
- ✓ also
- ✓ although
- ✓ and so on and so forth
- ✓ anyway
- ✓ appear
- ✓ approximately
- ✓ as a matter of fact
- ✓ back
- ✓ be able to
- ✓ began
- ✓ began to
- ✓ big
- ✓ bit
- ✓ by means of
- ✓ close
- ✓ down
- ✓ enough
- ✓ even
- ✓ ever
- ✓ every
- ✓ far
- ✓ feel
- ✓ for the most part
- ✓ going to
- ✓ have got
- ✓ however

- ✓ immediately
- ✓ important
- ✓ in order to
- ✓ indeed
- ✓ instinctively
- ✓ just
- ✓ just then
- ✓ like
- ✓ many
- ✓ might
- ✓ more or less
- ✓ most
- ✓ mused
- ✓ nearly
- ✓ never
- ✓ often
- ✓ only
- ✓ over
- ✓ own
- ✓ pretty
- ✓ quite
- ✓ rather
- ✓ real
- ✓ really
- ✓ roughly
- ✓ seem
- ✓ small
- ✓ so
- ✓ some
- ✓ somehow
- ✓ somewhat

- ✓ sort
- ✓ started
- ✓ started to
- ✓ still
- ✓ suddenly
- ✓ that
- ✓ then
- ✓ think
- ✓ though
- ✓ thought
- ✓ up
- ✓ used to
- ✓ usually
- ✓ very
- ✓ well
- ✓ wondered

Step 5

You can do this step in two different ways depending on your word processing program and how you prefer to work. We're going to be looking for helping and state-of-being verbs.

Option A

Run a search for the words *is*, *was*, and *were*. For each result, ask yourself the following questions.

Am I reporting a fact? (E.g., "She was ugly.") If so, how could I give evidence instead? What carefully selected details would best lead readers to the correct conclusion? Is the detail I've chosen to use consistent with what my point-of-view character would notice?

Helping and state-of-being verbs can often be replaced by stronger, tighter verbs. For example...

Emily was walking to work.

Becomes...

Emily walked to work.

Can the helping or state-of-being verbs you've located be removed to make your writing tighter and stronger?

Option B

If you prefer to do this step by hand, print out a chapter of your book. Use a highlighter and highlight all of the helping or state-of-being verbs listed in this chapter.

Is your page littered with highlights? This can be an indication not only of telling, but also that you need to work on replacing helping or state-of-being verbs with stronger, tighter verbs.

For example...

Emily was walking to work.

Becomes...

Emily walked to work.

Can the helping or state-of-being verbs you've located be removed to make your writing tighter and stronger?

For the rest, are you reporting a fact? (E.g., "She was ugly.") If so, how can you give evidence instead? What carefully selected details would best lead readers to the correct conclusion? Is the detail you've chosen to use consistent with what your point-of-view character would notice?

Step 6

Use the Find feature to search for these unspecific words. Can you rewrite the sentence to make it stronger and clearer? If so, go for it.

- ✓ get/got
- ✓ things
- ✓ moved
- ✓ took
- ✓ looked

PART THREE

Grammar Rules Every Writer Needs to Know and Follow

CHAPTER TWELVE

Passive Voice vs. Active Voice

You might remember this one from your high school or college English class days. I suspect that most of us at one point received an essay back with the comment "You used too much passive voice" accompanied by a lot of red circles.

Unfortunately, most of the time, these instructors forgot to explain to us what, exactly, a passive sentence was and why it was such a bad thing. My guess is they assumed we already knew.

If what I've seen in my editing work is any indication, many writers don't.

So let me explain to you what we mean when we talk about active vs. passive voice and why we should avoid it.

WHAT IS PASSIVE VOICE VS. ACTIVE VOICE?

Remember that the subject of a verb is the one who is doing or taking on the action of the verb.

When we use the *active voice*, the subject of the sentence is doing an action, or doing something to someone/something else.

When we use the *passive voice*, the subject of the sentence is the recipient of an action.

This is easier to see through examples. I'll put the subject of the sentences in bold.

> Passive: **They** were told by the lifeguard that the pool was closed.

> Active: The **lifeguard** told them that the pool was closed.

They are the subject in the passive sentence, but they're not doing anything. They're passive. They're being acted upon.

> Passive: The missing **boy** was located, cold and shivering, by the dauntless rescue team.

> Active: The dauntless rescue **team** located the cold, shivering missing boy.

The missing boy is the subject of the passive sentence, but he's not doing anything. Something is being done to him.

Fixing a use of passive voice might sound difficult, but it's actually pretty simple. Just make sure that the subject of the sentence (the noun that comes before the verb) is the one doing something. You'll know you're on the right track here if the verb is a single action verb that doesn't use any helping verbs (e.g., *was* or *were*).

WHY IS PASSIVE VOICE A PROBLEM?

Reason #1 - Compared to active voice, passive voice is wordy.

The tighter our writing, the faster it feels like the story is moving. It's a subliminal trick, but it works.

Beyond this, when we're writing, we often have word count limits placed on us. If we know that the typical romantic suspense novel is 75,000 to 80,000 words, we want to use those words on things that move the story forward and give the reader the best possible experience. We don't want to waste them writing something in eleven words when nine would do.

> Passive: The plant-closing notice was tacked on the bulletin board by Frank.

> Active: Frank tacked the plant-closing notice on the bulletin board.

Reason #2 – Passive voice feels awkward because it reverses the way people naturally think about things.

If you were thinking about the car that ran your spouse off the road, you wouldn't normally say...

> Jack was almost run off the road by that idiot.

You'd more naturally say...

> That idiot almost ran Jack off the road.

You wouldn't think...

> My clothes were shredded by the cat.

You'd think...

The cat shredded my clothes.

You wouldn't think...

A dead frog was left in front of my door by my landlord.

You'd probably think...

My landlord left a dead frog in front of my door.

Human beings tend to think first about the thing acting rather than about the thing being acted on.

Reason #3 – The reader can get confused by the delay in naming the actor.

Let's go back to our sentence about the dead frog.

The dead frog was left in front of my door by the next-door neighbor that wants to get rid of me.

The dead frog was left in front of my door by my landlord.

We don't find out who put the dead frog in front of the door until the end of the sentence. That gives the reader time to make an assumption and be wrong, especially if the actor will be someone they didn't expect.

Reason #4 – Active voice makes the reader feel more like they're experiencing the action along with the character.

You can see this one best if we look at an example.

Passive: The giant boulder was rolled in front of the cave entrance by Frank.

You're separated from Frank. This sentence feels distant and disconnected.

> Active: Frank rolled the giant bolder in front of the cave entrance.

With the active version, it feels more like we're watching it happen in front of us rather than being told about it secondhand. We're there with Frank.

SHOULD WE EVER USE PASSIVE VOICE?

I'm glad you asked, because the answer is *yes*.

If you don't know who the subject (the actor) is, you'll have to use the passive voice.

> Example: Our car was set on fire.

You might (notice I said *might*) also want to use the passive voice if the person who did the action is less important than the action itself. This is an option we have, but we still need to use it wisely and sparingly.

CHAPTER THIRTEEN

Subject-Verb Agreement

One grammar rule that absolutely can't be broken is proper subject–verb agreement. Basically, this means that the verb form changes based on whether the subject of the sentence is singular or plural. This is nonnegotiable, as improper subject–verb agreement can actually make your writing silly and/or unintelligible.

We'll start with an example that everyone who speaks English as their first language would get just so you can see what I mean by subject-verb agreement. I've italicized the subject and put the verb in bold.

Incorrect: *They* **is** happy.

Is they really? *They* is a plural pronoun, so the verb needs to be plural.

Correct: *They* **are** happy.

Now that you know what I mean when I say subject–verb agreement, we can move on to the ones that even native English speakers bungle.

<u>Incorrect</u>: The number of people at the music festival **are** growing.

This is a fairly common mistake because we focus on the word *people*, which is actually the object of the preposition and has no bearing on the correct verb use.

A preposition is put before a noun or pronoun to show the (pro)noun's relationship to another word in the sentence. So in our example above, *of* is the preposition that connects *number* and *people*. Number of what? Number of people.

To find the subject of a sentence that includes one or more prepositional phrases (the phrases that follow prepositions), just mentally delete the prepositional phrase.

Think of it this way. Your sentence is like an ice cream sundae. The base sentence is the ice cream. Everything else is nuts and whip cream and hot fudge. When someone asks you what type of ice cream you have, they want to know the flavor of the ice cream, not all the other stuff. To see what flavor of ice cream you have, you need to strip away everything that's not ice cream.

So let's go back to our original example.

<u>Incorrect</u>: The number of people at the music festival are growing.

If you're still confused about how to figure out what's the subject and what's the prepositional phrase, try deleting both.

The people at the music festival are growing.

Umm, unless the people are all children or they're eating Alice in Wonderland's growth cake, that's probably not what you mean.

Let's try again.

The number at the music festival is growing.

We still have to ask ourselves *number of what?* But that's where we can answer *of people.*

> Correct: The number of people at the music festival *is* growing.

Let's look at another, more complex, example of this.

> The number of members of Congress with a good approval rating is low.

In the sentence above, we actually have three prepositional phrases: *of members, of Congress,* and *with a good approval rating.* If we mentally delete these, we're left with "The *number is* low."

How do we know those are the prepositional phrases?

They all describe another word in the sentence.

The number of what? Of members.

Members of what? Of Congress.

What type of members of Congress? The ones with a good approval rating.

So all that can go, leaving us with...

> The number is low.

This is a very important aspect of writing, for both fiction and nonfiction, and not using correct subject–verb agreement can result in people putting down your work and never picking up anything else you ever write.

And here's another reason it's important. If you want to write a character whose first language isn't English, a subtle way to make their dialogue unique is to give them problems with subject-verb agreement. Many people who speak English as a second language struggle with subject-verb agreement even in simple sentences.

When you understand it, you can play with it in a character that doesn't.

CHAPTER FOURTEEN

Double Negatives

A double negative is when you use two negative terms side by side. Negative terms include *don't, can't, won't, aren't, not,* and so on.

They are generally used to indicate—you guessed it—that something didn't happen or something wasn't said.

Unfortunately, a double negative does just the opposite. It indicates that something actually did happen or actually was said because the negatives cancel each other out.

Take the example below:

> I didn't not say I don't like pizza.

What you're actually saying, since *don't* is a contraction of *do not,* is "I did not not say I do not like pizza," which is confusing.

The correct way to say this is "I didn't say I don't like pizza," or even "I never said I don't like pizza."

Let's look at another one.

> I don't not like pizza.

What you're actually saying, since *don't* is a contraction of *do not*, is "I do not not like pizza," or, more simply, "I like pizza."

If you don't like pizza, you'd say, "I don't like pizza."

No matter what happens, it's not never a good time to use double negatives, because if you don't not never use double negatives, your reader won't not never understand what you're not not saying.

See what we did there? We'd say that the sentence above is about as clear as mud, wouldn't you? Using double negatives makes your writing confusing. Unless you're writing a riddle, you should always strive to be as clear as possible in your writing, so that your readers have no trouble understanding you. If your readers don't understand what you're trying to say, they won't *remain* your readers.

CHAPTER FIFTEEN

Don't Get Tense

D id you know that there are no fewer than 15 tenses?

For most fiction writers, the important decision about tenses will be choosing whether to write in present tense or past tense. Both are now acceptable, and many popular books— like *The Hunger Games* and *The Help*—have been written in present tense.

But on a smaller, sentence-by-sentence level, there's more to tenses than just present and past tense.

In this chapter, we're going to walk you through the different types of tenses and explain when to use them in your novel, as well as when to avoid them.

SIMPLE

The simple tenses are the simple past, simple present, and simple future. The simple tenses are the backbone of good fiction.

> She ate the moldy bread. (Past)
> She eats the moldy bread. (Present)
> She will eat the moldy bread. (Future)

She is going to eat the moldy bread. (Future)

(And we're betting she felt pretty sick afterward.)

As we mentioned in the introduction to this chapter, your foundational choices for writing your novel are to write in the past tense or the present tense. Unless you're writing experimental fiction, the action of your novel, the meat of what's happening in your plot, won't be taking place in the future tense.

That doesn't mean the future tense is useless. For example, you might have one character say to another "We will walk to the park tomorrow whether you like it or not."

PROGRESSIVE

Progressive tenses give us a sense of a continuing action. They're ongoing. Something was happening in the past, is currently happening, or will be happening in the future.

> She was walking. (Past progressive)
> She is walking. (Present progressive)
> She will be walking. (Future progressive)

The problem with progressive tense in fiction is that you normally don't need it. Fiction readers have been conditioned to understand that when you write something like "She walked down the street," the implication is that she's walking until you say she isn't anymore. You don't need to write "She was walking." In fact, you shouldn't write "She was walking." It's considered wordy.

The exception is the future progressive. Let's say your characters are planning a bank heist. You might have a situation where one says to the other...

> "The guard will be walking to the elevator at 8:30 sharp.
> That's your only chance to catch him alone."

CONDITIONAL

Conditional tenses deal with things that may or may not have happened. You can tell a conditional tense by the word *would*. You'll also find them in "if-then" type statements.

As fiction writers, we're most likely to use the conditional tense in internal dialogue or when a character is planning for the future.

> Alan **would** be meeting with clients from one o'clock until three. It **would** be her only opportunity to hack the safe, steal her passport, and escape from him for good.

> Bruce pulled out of the driveway, glancing in the rearview mirror to make sure no one was following him. He **wouldn't** put it past Elaine to hire a PI to trail him. If she caught him with Rebecca, **he'd** have no choice but to admit the truth.

The trick with the conditional tense is to make sure we don't use it for too many sentences in a row. Our characters need to stay firmly grounded in acting in the present. We can't allow them to ponder what could be or to be locked up in their own heads for too long.

PERFECT AND PERFECT PROGRESSIVE

You won't use the perfect tense (or the related perfect progressive) as often as the other tenses, but that doesn't mean they're not important.

The perfect tense focuses on the result of a completed action or on the fact that an action has taken place.

You know you have the perfect tense if the sentence includes the words *had* or *have* paired with a past-tense verb (e.g., *walked, talked, eaten, shown*).

> I had eaten frog legs. (Past perfect)

I have eaten frog legs. (Present perfect)
I will have eaten frog legs. (Future perfect)

(And it tasted just like chicken. Isn't that what they say about everything?)

Perfect progressive is very similar. You'll know a perfect progressive because it combines *had been* or *have been* with the ongoing form of the verb (usually an *–ing*). The idea behind the perfect progressive is of an action with duration or a length to it.

I had been eating frog legs. (Past perfect progressive)
I have been eating frog legs. (Present perfect progressive)
I will have been eating frog legs. (Future perfect progressive)

Perfect and past perfect are so closely related that it's easiest to discuss them together.

The problem with the perfect tense is that many writers will use it when they don't need to.

The right way to use the perfect tense is if we want to quickly telescope time rather than slowing the story down to show it happening blow by blow.

By the time they reached the haunted cemetery, the rain had begun falling.

I'll give you another example so you can see this more clearly. You have two dating characters who were delayed by a flat tire and had a fight over it. You could describe them reaching the movie theater and trying to get in, only to find out that they'd missed the movie entirely. But it's likely that the actual details of finding out the movie is already over aren't important. What *was* important was the flat tire and the fight and the fallout that will happen after finding out the movie is over and they missed it. In this case, instead of wasting a page or more on them finding out the movie is over, you could write...

> By the time they reached the theater, the movie had ended.

You could also safely use the perfect tense when you have one character telling another about something they did in the past. (You're using past perfect tense.)

> Lenny stared at her, his eyes reminding her of a shark's. *"I've killed* before. I'll do it again."

The part in bold is present perfect.

Another appropriate way to use the perfect tense is to signal a flashback or memory.

> He'd never forget the day he met her. He had been shopping for flowers to send his mother on the first anniversary of his father's death, and Emily's flower shop was across the street from the courthouse where he worked.

In this example, the perfect progressive signals to the reader that a flashback is coming. In a longer flashback, you'll use the perfect progressive to transition into it and then go back into the simple past tense. When you want to come out of the flashback, you'll need to signal the reader again, either by a line break or by using the trigger of mentioning something you mentioned right before going into the flashback.

I'll give you an example.

> Rick pulled up to the wrought-iron gate at the address he'd tricked the school secretary into giving him.

He rang the buzzer. A lot must have changed for Emily in the ten years since they'd said goodbye.

He'd never forget the day he met her. He had been shopping for flowers to send his mother on the first anniversary of his father's death, and Emily's flower shop was across the street from the courthouse where he worked.

He wandered around the shop for fifteen minutes, his lunch hour slipping away.

Emily craned her head around a shelf of ribbons. "Are you sure there's nothing I can help you with?"

(And then you continue with your flashback.)

The intercom next to the gate crackled to life. "Yes?"

The perfect tense has many viable, important uses in fiction.

But here's where perfect tense can weigh you down—if it destroys the sense of immediacy in your story. Creating a sense of watching things happen in real time, giving a sense of immediacy, can be difficult enough in past-tense writing. It gets worse when you write something like this...

> She had double-checked that all the windows were locked, and had set the alarm before leaving the house.

We're being told something happened. We're not seeing it play out on the page in front of us. The simple solution to make this showing rather than telling, and to allow the reader to feel like it's happening, is to change it to a simple past tense.

> She double-checked that all the windows were locked, and set the alarm, before leaving the house.

It says the same thing, but it feels more immediate and the writing is tighter. Never use the past perfect when the simple past tense will do.

When it comes to tenses, you don't need to try to remember what each tense is called. The important thing to understand and remember is what each tense is used for and the potential pitfalls you need to be aware of.

CHAPTER SIXTEEN

Lack of Parallelism

A lack of parallelism is important to snuff out because it can result in funny sentences. It's also important because parallelism in lists makes your writing more beautiful to read and easier to understand.

Here's a sentence lacking parallelism.

> To contribute to Easter dinner, Lillian peeled two potatoes, three yams, and baked a pie.

Your reader will understand this sentence, but it will feel awkward. And grammar Nazis will snicker at you behind their hands.

Take the sentence apart and you'll see the problem.

> To contribute to Easter dinner, Lillian . . .
> **peeled** two potatoes
> three yams
> **baked** a pie

You wouldn't say, "To contribute to Easter dinner, Lillian three yams." At least, I hope you wouldn't. It sounds like it belongs in a spoof of *Top Gun*.

"What's your name?"

"Lillian Threeyams."

"Threeyams? Did your parents not like you or something?"

You need to add a verb in front of *three yams* to make this sentence parallel. *Peeled, washed, chopped,* or *mashed* would all be correct.

To contribute to Easter dinner, Lillian peeled two potatoes, cleaned three yams, and baked a pie.

You'll most likely see lists in fiction in the form of the sentence above. For those of you who also write nonfiction, watch your bullet-point lists—this applies to them as well. Take each piece of your list and read it alone with the opening. Does it work? Or do you end up with a "Lillian three yams" atrocity?

CHAPTER SEVENTEEN

Woe Is Me: Dealing With I/Me, Who/Whom, and That/Which/Who

grouped these issues into one lesson because you'll find some similarities in what's actually causing the problem and how to fix it. Even though each of these could be a lesson in themselves, I felt that bringing them together in one place would be easier for you.

Before we jump into sorting through I/me and who/whom, we need to have a refresher about *subjects and objects* and *passive voice vs. active voice.*

Back in the chapter on commas, we talked about the subject of a sentence. We also talked about how complete sentences need to contain a subject and a predicate.

Now we're going to talk about the verbs in a sentence and how verbs have both a subject and an object. (Remember that the verb is just part of the predicate.)

The subject of a verb, just like the subject of a sentence, is always going to be a noun (person, place, thing, or state of being) or pronoun (a word, like *he* or *it*, that stands in for a noun).

When it comes to the subject and object of a verb, the subject is the one taking on or doing the action of the verb.

In an active sentence, the subject of the verb does the action. In a passive sentence, the subject of the verb takes on an action.

Below I've underlined the verb and placed the subject in bold. Both of these are in the active voice.

> **I** <u>love</u> my husband.
>
> **My cat** <u>licks</u> her fur.

The object of the verb is the person or thing having the action done to them. Below I've identified these in our examples in italics.

> **I** <u>love</u> *my husband.*
>
> **My cat** <u>licks</u> *her fur.*

Now I'm going to write our above examples in the passive voice and highlight the different parts the same way as above (subject in bold, verb underlined, and object in italics) so you can see what happens.

> **My husband** <u>is loved</u> *by me.*
>
> **My cat's fur** <u>is licked</u> *by my cat.*

You might remember that we call these sentences *passive* because the subjects of the verbs are lazy. They're not doing anything. They're taking on the verb, having something done to them.

Whether we're writing fiction or nonfiction, we want to write in the active voice as much as possible.

But here are two things I want you to remember.

A sentence using a "to be" verb isn't necessarily passive.

I've underlined the *to be* construction in the following example.

> *Active:* I <u>am holding</u> my husband's hand.
> *Passive:* My husband's hand <u>is held</u> by me.

This sentence uses a weak verb, but it can have both a passive and an active form without removing the *to be* construction.

In English, the subject of the sentence is largely determined by its position relative to the verb.

The subject comes before the verb in most cases.

Exception #1 – Questions

Not all questions will invert the natural order, but some will.

> Are neither my wishes nor my goals important?

If you're confused by the subject and object in a question, turn it into an answer to the question.

> No, your wishes and your goals aren't important.

The compound subject is *wishes and goals*. (And if your spouse ever says this to you, you'll be headed for counseling.)

Exception #2 – Sentences opening with phrases such as "there are" or "it is"

> There is nothing to be gained from lying.

The subject is *nothing*. You could reword the sentence as *Nothing is gained from lying.*

Here are the copies you asked for.

The subject is *copies*. You could reword the sentence as *The copies you asked for are here.*

Exception #3 – When you say what was done before you say who did it

Walking around the yard were two dogs.

Walking can't be the subject of the sentence because it's not a noun or a pronoun.

The subject is *dogs*.

Two dogs were walking around the yard.

I know that was a lot to take in, but now I can explain how we decide whether to use *I* or *me* and *who* or *whom*.

I is used as the subject. *Me* is used as the object.

Who is used as the subject. *Whom* is used as the object.

It sounds easy when parsed down that way, but it can be a little trickier in execution in certain situations, so let me walk you through it.

I/ME

There are two tricky cases when it comes to figuring out whether to use *I* or *me*.

The first is when you have a compound subject/object.

Which do you think is correct?

A - She loves you and I equally.

B - She loves you and me equally.

Your instinct is likely to say A is correct because we've been somehow trained to think that *I* is the cultured choice. But the correct answer is B.

Look what happens when we do this...

A – She loves ~~you and~~ I ~~equally~~.

B – She loves ~~you and~~ me ~~equally~~.

You'd never dream of saying "She loves I" (at least not if you want anyone to understand you) so you shouldn't say "She loves you and I."

The second is following a preposition.

Prepositions are position words (e.g., *after, at, before, between, by, for, from, in, like, on, toward, with*).

We have the same knee-jerk reaction following a preposition as we do with a compound object following a verb. We want to put an *I*.

Guess again.

A – The odds were against you and I.

B – The odds were against you and me.

You should know how to figure this out now.

A – The odds were against ~~you and~~ I.

B – The odds were against ~~you and~~ me.

IT IS I – AN EXCEPTION TO THE RULE

Technically speaking, when a pronoun follows a *to be* verb, it should act as a subject. Consequently, generations were taught to say "It is I" and "This is she."

And while "It is I" is still correct, "It's me" is now common parlance and, unless you're trying to characterize an English teacher, someone from a past era of history, etc., you'll want to use "It's me," not "It is I," in your fiction.

WHO/WHOM

Who is used as a subject. *Whom* is used as an object.

A little trick to remember this is that you use *who* in the same place you would use *he* or *they*. You use *whom* in the same place you would use *him* or *them*. Notice how all three words in the second sentence end in *m*.

Unfortunately, it can sometimes still be tricky to figure out which one you need. Here's how to solve the problem.

When "who/whom" appears in a question

Did I tell you who/whom I saw at the store?

All you have to do for this is frame it as an answer.

I saw him at the store.

Therefore...

Did I tell you whom I saw at the store?

When "who/whom" appears buried in other words

We only invited guests to the party who/whom we thought would have fun.

You could rearrange the words the same way you did with a question…

We thought <u>they</u> would have fun.

But it's easier to just cut the fluff around the clause (subject + predicate clasped together) in a question.

We only invited guests to the party <u>who/whom</u> ~~we thought~~ would have fun.

That makes it clear that the clause has *who/whom* as the subject.

<u>Who</u> would have fun.

Therefore…

We only invited guests to the party <u>who</u> we thought would have fun.

I'll show you another one.

Bob wouldn't tell his girlfriend <u>who/whom</u> he invited to his poker game.

Aside from the fact that Bob probably won't have a girlfriend much longer, we can also remove the words around the clause in question…

~~Bob wouldn't tell his girlfriend~~ who/whom he invited ~~to his poker game~~.

When you cut away everything else like this, you can see that *who/whom* isn't doing the inviting. *He* did the inviting. *Who/whom* is the one being invited.

Therefore…

Bob wouldn't tell his girlfriend <u>whom</u> he invited to his poker game.

DOES IT MATTER WHETHER YOU USE "WHO" OR "WHOM"?

Sometimes it does, but not usually. If you're writing a blog post, you can feel safe using *who*, regardless of whether it's the subject or the object. The same thing goes for fiction.

With two qualifications.

If you use *whom*, you need to make sure you're using it correctly. (In other words, don't put *whom* where *who* actually belongs.)

Knowing the difference between *who* and *whom* gives you a way to set apart the dialogue of a well-educated or pretentious character from an average Joe. Use it well.

THAT/WHICH/WHO

We're in the home stretch of the chapter now, and this part is much easier.

When should we use "that" and when should we use "who"?

Tim is the man <u>who/that</u> my cousin married.

The answer is simpler than you might think.

A person can technically be a *who* or a *that*, but the preference is to always refer to human beings as *who*.

A thing is always a *that*.

The lines turn gray when you're talking about animals, but the general guideline is that an animal is a *that* if it's unnamed and a *who* if its named or directly connected to a person (e.g., *my cat who, my dog who*).

There's the dog <u>that</u> works with the police by sniffing out bombs.

Luna is a dog <u>who</u> loves her food.

When should we use "that" and when should we use "which"?

Use *which* if the clause is non-restrictive and *that* if the clause is restrictive.

I know—time for some more definitions. Once you get the hang of these, I promise you can forget all the terms because you'll know how to apply these concepts, and that's all that really matters.

A *clause* includes both a subject and a predicate.

To help you remember that a <u>clause</u> requires both a subject and a predicate, think about <u>clasping</u> your hands together. <u>C</u>lause = <u>c</u>lasp.

A clause can be either dependent or independent, but you'll only run into the *that/which* conundrum in dependent clauses. (Remember, dependent clauses are ones that can't stand alone as a sentence.)

Dependent clauses come in two types.

A ***non-restrictive clause*** is one that the sentence doesn't need to make sense. It merely provides additional information about a subject that's already been clearly identified. The non-restrictive clause in the sentence below is underlined and bolded.

My cat, ***<u>who is black and wears a red collar</u>***, likes to sleep on the window ledge.

You can remove the underlined portion without changing the meaning of the sentence and without it being any less clear.

My cat likes to sleep on the window ledge.

A ***restrictive clause*** is one the sentence needs. It won't make sense or won't say the same thing without it. It restricts the meaning in some sense. The restrictive clause in the sentence below is under-lined.

> The cat ***that lives with my neighbor*** likes to catch birds in
> my yard.

Look what happens when you remove the restrictive clause.

> The cat likes to catch birds in my yard.

What cat?

Look at another example.

> The spider ***that spins those webs*** is poisonous.

Try taking the restrictive clause out and see how ambiguous the sentence becomes.

> The spider is poisonous.

If you're me, you're asking "Which spider?" in a panicky voice and are looking for the heaviest possible object to throw at it. Those *that* clauses can be mighty important.

Now let's look at how this applies to choosing between *that* and *which*.

> Tomatoes, ***which come in red and green varieties***, are ac-tually fruits, not vegetables.

This is non-restrictive—we could remove it and the subject would still be clear, so we use *which*. Now look what happens in a restrictive clause where we need that element to make sense.

> The tomato ***that you threw at me*** left a bruise on my
> cheek.

Because it's restrictive, we need to use *that*.

If you're British or Australian, the rules might be slightly different. For this one, I recommend that you either look at some of the traditionally published books on your shelf or check out a grammar guide written specifically for your country.

CHAPTER EIGHTEEN

Take It to the Page: Part Three

As you become more comfortable with grammar, you'll find that you make fewer and fewer mistakes in your writing. However, even once we're comfortable with the rules and guidelines of English grammar, it can help to have quick ways to check some of the most common glips.

Step 1

Back in the Take It to the Page section for Part Two, you did a search for helping and state-of-being verbs. One of those verbs was *was*. We're going to search for it again. Because you removed many of the instances of it before, this search should be quicker. This time, when you see a *was*, check if the sentence is passive. Would it be stronger if you rewrote it as an active sentence? If so, rewrite it. If not, make sure you wrote it as a passive sentence either purposefully or because there was no better way to write it. (Reminder: If you're writing in present tense, you'll need to search for *is* instead.)

Step 2

Use the Find feature to search for *had* and *would*. If you want, you can use the Find and Replace feature to replace *had* with *HAD* and *would* with *WOULD* to help them stand out better. If you see these words too many times, it can indicate you're using the perfect tense and/or the perfect progressive tense too often.

Check to see if the *HAD* sentences could be changed to simple past tense.

Check to see if you can remove some of the repetitive *WOULD* sentences by rewriting them.

Step 3

Use the Find feature to search for *whom*. Should it be *who*? (We're not going to run a search for *who*. *Who* is now commonly accepted as a stand-in for *whom*. We *are* searching for *whom*, however, because, if you're going to use it, you need to be sure you use it correctly.)

Step 4

Run a search for the following words.

- ✓ That – Should it be *who* or *which* instead? Is this a leftover weasel word that you should cut?
- ✓ Who – Should it be *that* or *which* instead?
- ✓ Which – Should it be *who* or *that* instead?

PART FOUR

Special Challenges for Fiction Writers

CHAPTER NINETEEN

Dangling Participles and Misplaced Modifiers

Your readers will find you extremely funny for all the wrong reasons if you leave your participles dangling and your modifiers misplaced.

In this chapter, I need to define a few grammatical terms for you so that you can easily spot and fix problem sentences. I'll keep it as straightforward as possible, only delving in to what you need to know. Hang in there. It'll be worth it. (Or, at the very least, it'll give you a great excuse to eat some chocolate to feel better afterward.)

Remember, every complete sentence needs two things: a *subject* and a *predicate*. Because of how important this is, I'm going to cover it quickly again.

The **subject** is the thing the sentence is about. (Think "test subject" in an experiment.)

> *I* am tired of hearing about subjects and predicates.
> *My black cat* caught a mouse for me.
> *Emily and Bob's house* fell down.
> *Mosquitoes* bite.

The *predicate* tells us something about the subject. It might tell us what the subject did, what it looks like, etc. (I like to remember this as a friend of *prediction*, which tells us something about the future.)

> I ***am tired of hearing about subjects and predicates***.
> My black cat ***caught a mouse for me***.
> Emily and Bob's house ***fell down***.
> Mosquitoes ***bite***.

The important thing to remember about the predicate is that it contains a *verb*. (A verb describes an action, state of being, or relationship between two things.)

> I ***am tired*** of hearing about subjects and predicates.
> My black cat ***caught*** a mouse for me.
> Emily and Bob's house ***fell*** down.
> Mosquitoes ***bite***.

All a predicate needs to be complete is a verb (as you can see in the last example.)

Now here's where it gets a little more complicated, because we need to talk about independent clauses, dependent clauses, and phrases.

These are all parts of a sentence. Think of the sentence like a book, and these other things are like chapters and scenes.

Any time you put a subject and a predicate together, you have a *clause*.

An *independent clause* can stand alone. This should make sense if you think about an independent person. They like to do things on their own.

> My husband is an editor.
> I walked to the store.

Both of these are independent clauses because they're complete sentences. The underlined part below is also an independent clause.

As I walked to the store, *I saw a deer*.

We call the underlined part independent because, if we took it out of the sentence, it still makes sense. Like this...

I saw a deer.

Think of independent clauses like chapters within a book that could be a complete short story on their own, and which would make sense even if you removed them from the book.

A *dependent clause* needs something else to complete it. (Just like a dependent person needs someone else's emotional or physical support.)

As I walked to the store, I saw a deer.

If you separate out the underlined part, you should instinctively sense that something is missing.

As I walked to the store,

You feel like you should ask "What happened?" It doesn't make any sense on its own. It needs the rest of the sentence.

Think of dependent clauses like chapters within a book that wouldn't make sense if you removed them from the context of the rest of the story.

Notice how both the dependent and independent clauses contain a subject (underlined) and a predicate (bolded and italicized).

As I *walked to the store*, I *saw a deer*.

Remember that a <u>clause</u> requires both a subject and a predicate. <u>C</u>lause = <u>c</u>lasp.

A **phrase** is a related group of words that doesn't qualify as a clause because it's missing either a subject or a predicate. I've underlined the phrase in the sentence below.

I walked **_to the store_**.

I know this might seem confusing because earlier I said that *to the store* was part of the predicate. And it is—but it isn't the whole predicate.

Think of the phrase like a scene contributing to a bigger chapter in a book.

So now we're ready to move on to spotting out-of-place modifiers.

A **modifier** describes or qualifies another element within the sentence.

We run into the problem of dangling participles and misplaced modifiers because, unlike other languages, in English, the role a word plays in a sentence is determined by its location, rather than by a change in the ending.

DANGLING PARTICIPLES

A participle is just the *–ing* form of a verb.

Walk (verb) → walking (present participle)
Fall (verb) → falling (present participle)
Laugh (verb) → laughing (present participle)

A participle can take part in a participial phrase that modifies a noun. The participial phrase is underlined below.

Hiking the trail, I felt a sense of peace.

See how it doesn't have a subject, so it's a phrase (not a clause), and it's a participial phrase because it uses a participle (the –*ing* form of a verb). Easier than you thought, right?

A participial phrase needs to bond to a subject noun. If you don't provide it with a proper one, it'll bond to whatever noun is closest. The result is like when a duckling imprints on a dog.

When that happens, we call it a dangling participial. A ***dangling participle*** is a participle or a participial phrase that modifies the wrong noun. It attempts to modify something that isn't the proper subject of the sentence.

> Walking down the road, the house came into view.

A house taking a walk? I'd buy tickets to see that.

> Featuring a hot tub and extra-fluffy pillows, we highly recommend this hotel's suites for honeymooning couples.

The mental image of people with hot tubs where their bellies should be and pillows for arms... I probably won't stop laughing long enough to read the rest of what you've written. You'll see sentences like that one all the time on travel sites, but that doesn't make it right.

Here's another one.

> After rotting in the back of the fridge for three months, my husband cleaned out his forgotten leftovers.

Based on this sentence, I need to take my husband to a doctor to find out why he's rotting.

How could we fix these?

Wrong:

Walking down the road, the house came into view.

Correction:

We could change the participial phrase into a dependent clause so...

As we walked down the road, the house came into view.

Correction:

We could break the sentence into two independent clauses.

We walked down the road, and the house came into view.

MISPLACED MODIFIERS

Remember that a dangling participle makes the wrong noun the subject of the sentence.

A misplaced modifier is a modifier that describes or qualifies something other than what we want it to.

As a soccer mom, Ellen's van was always full of boys.

A van that can procreate. Will medical marvels never cease?

Correct Version: As a soccer mom, Ellen found her van was always full of boys.

Also Correct: Always full of boys, Ellen's van marked her as a soccer mom.

Let me give you another example.

Overweight and balding, the vet says our cat might have hormone problems.

Is your cat overweight and balding, or is your vet overweight and balding? Because in this sentence, it's your vet, and I have to wonder what that has to do with your cat's hormone problems.

> Corrected Version: The vet says that our cat's balding and excessive weight could be symptoms of hormone problems.

Now it's clear that your cat is the fat, balding one. And you won't accidentally insult your vet.

One more example before we move on. Misplaced modifiers can come in many forms, and I don't want you to think they only happen when a comma is involved. They can sneak themselves into the middle of a sentence as well.

> Leaning over the body, she looked into the empty man's eyes.

How does she know the man is empty? Has he been gutted?

> Corrected Version: Leaning over the body, she looked into the man's empty eyes.

In this version, it's clear that his eyes are empty of life.

CONFUSED MODIFIERS

A confused modifier is something that could modify more than one thing in the sentence. Consequently, the meaning of the sentence is unclear.

> My boss said on Friday we'd have to stay late.

On Friday could be modifying when the boss spoke or when they'd have to work late.

Depending on which meaning you intended, you'd rewrite the sentence to read...

On Friday, my boss said we'd have to work late.

My boss said we'd have to work late on Friday.

Let's look at another example.

The boy who was profiled in the local newspaper recently had a chance to meet his hero.

Was he recently profiled in the newspaper or did he recently have a chance to meet his hero? This sentence could mean either. Here's how you could fix this depending on what you meant.

The boy who was recently profiled in the local newspaper had a chance to meet his hero.

The boy who was profiled in the local newspaper had a chance to meet his hero recently.

The real trouble with confused modifiers is that, if we happen to read the sentence the intended way, we don't realize anything is wrong. The key is to train ourselves to recognize when the modifier is unclear and also to have a second person go over our work whenever possible.

CHAPTER TWENTY

Reversing Cause and Effect

A common mistake made by fiction writers is the reversal of the necessary order of cause coming before effect, action coming before reaction.

In science fiction, you might deal with a temporal paradox. In real life, cause always comes before effect. The effect can't come before what caused it.

Unfortunately, we can easily reverse them unintentionally in our writing for many reasons. Perhaps we're trying to add variety to our sentences and we don't think about what we're accidentally doing.

When you reverse the two so that the effect comes first, your readers will feel thrown off-balance and disconnected from your writing, even if they can't always tell you why.

The easiest way to spot this happening is to look for the words *as, while,* and *when.*

They're often used as connections between things that are supposed to be happening at the same time. Often they're not actually happening at the same time. Often, you're messing up your cause and effect.

Let me give you an example of what I mean.

As the shot rang out, Ellen covered her ears.

No, she didn't. Not unless she's psychic. She couldn't have done what the sentence says because, until she heard the shot, Ellen had no reason to cover her ears.

The shot rang out, and Ellen covered her ears.

Let me give you a look at another way this could appear.

He blushed as he realized his fly was undone.

Blushing is the result or effect of realizing his fly is undone. This sentence feels odd because the cause and effect are flipped. He realizes his fly is undone, and as a result, his face heats. (*Realized* is a dangerous word in our fiction for other reasons as well. If you'd like to learn more, check out *Mastering Showing and Telling in Your Fiction: A Busy Writer's Guide.*)

I'll give you another example using *when* instead.

We took cover when we heard him entering the building.

They didn't take cover at the same time as they heard him entering. Until they heard him entering, they had no reason to take cover. First they heard him entering, and then, as a consequence of hearing it, they took cover.

Even if you do have two things that actually happen at the same time, you should try to avoid connecting them with *as* because the reader's experience isn't "at the same time." Their experience is linear. Because of the nature of reading, we can't experience two things at the same time. We experience them in the order they appear on the page. For this reason, you're best to put the action that ends quickest first and then connect them with a different conjunction.

A corollary of this is when you create a sentence where you're not suggesting things are happening at the same time, but you've still reversed the natural order. Once again, we'll look at an example so you can see what I mean.

> My mouth went dry and a heavy weight settled in my chest as he led me down the hall to meet my birth mother for the first time.

Technically, this can be happening at the same time. This is one of those situations that can justify breaking the linear rule because walking down the hall takes time. There's time for something to happen as she's walking.

Here's the problem. Your sentence structure still needs to reflect the natural order. Even if you want to express that something is happening at the same time, when you write it, you need to give the reader the cause before you give them the effect.

In the above example, we find out our narrator's mouth is dry and she feels a heavy weight on her chest, but the reader will feel ungrounded because they have no idea what's causing it. Any time the reader loses connection to the POV character and immersion in the story, it's a bad thing.

You'll find this in your writing when your words express that one thing happened temporally before the other, but in the sentence you've reversed them. So you're saying A happened before B, but in your sentence what you've written is "B happened because of A."

You need to write down the cause (A) before the effect (B).

Before we move on, let's quickly go back to the example above and see one possible way we could rewrite it, keeping this in mind.

He led me down the hall to meet my birth mother. My mouth went dry and a heavy weight settled in my chest.

When you make sure that you've kept the natural order, you'll find you're also able to better avoid dangling participles and misplaced modifiers.

CHAPTER TWENTY-ONE

Are Your Characters Doing the Impossible?

Fixing this grammar mistake is extremely important for fiction writers. It might seem small, but if you don't catch it and correct it, it can leave your writing feeling awkward...and any reader who catches it will stumble over the sentence. This error is a close cousin to reversing cause and effect. As soon as I give you some examples, you'll start to see why.

It happens when we're trying to vary our sentence structure, and so we write an abomination like...

Rising from her chair, she walked across the room.

Was she glued to the chair? This sentence has her both rising from the chair and walking across the room at the same time. She can't do both at the same time. I'll give you another example.

Dropping to her knees, she scooped up the broken dish.

Again, she doesn't scoop up the dish while dropping to her knees. She drops to her knees, and then she scoops up the dish. It's not possible for her to be scooping up the dish until she's down where she can reach it.

When you've written a dependent clause and have connected it with a comma to an independent clause, check that the two actions can and do actually occur at the same time.

When you find actions that can't happen at the same time, the fix is simple. All you need to do is make them two sentences or connect the clauses with a conjunction like *and*.

> She rose from her chair and walked across the room.

> She dropped to her knees and scooped up the broken dish.

This holds true no matter what tense you're writing in.

> She rises from her chair and walks across the room.

> She drops to her knees and scoops up the broken dish.

Make sure that, when your characters act, it's something they could actually do. Unless, of course, you're writing a fantasy. In that case, you make your own rules about what's possible...but then you have to abide by those as well.

CHAPTER TWENTY-TWO

Orphaned Dialogue and Pronouns

The last special challenge for fiction writers that we need to look at is orphans. When I say *orphans*, I'm talking about pronouns that could refer to more than one person (and are thus unclaimed) and dialogue where we don't know for sure who's speaking.

You might occasionally run into a problem with orphaned pronouns when writing non-fiction, but, for the most part, these are both challenges unique to fiction writers.

ORPHANED PRONOUNS

An orphaned pronoun is a pronoun that's placed in a sentence in such a way that it's unclear which person or animal the pronoun refers to. It's not always difficult to figure out which pronoun refers to which person or animal, but orphaned pronouns don't really lend themselves to clear writing. They typically occur in sentences where two or more of characters in the sentence are of the same gender.

Example:
Jennifer's mom told her that she couldn't eat pizza.

Does the sentence mean that Jennifer's mom is prohibiting Jennifer from eating pizza, or does it mean that Jennifer's mom (we'll call her Tracy) is saying Tracy herself is unable to eat pizza for some reason?

Orphaned pronouns often happen because we're trying to avoid writing something awkward or wordy like...

Jennifer's mom told her that Jennifer couldn't eat pizza.

However, in most cases, if we look for a new way to write the sentence rather than just replacing the pronoun with a proper name, we can make it read smoothly and clearly.

Jennifer's mom shoved the box of frozen pizza back in the freezer. "I've already told you twice. No pizza."

Let's look at another example.

Jack's dad told him that his actions were unacceptable, and that he had to be more responsible in the future or he would be in serious trouble.

The end of the sentence seems to make it clear that Jack is in trouble, but we just don't know because the pronouns *him*, *his*, and *he* are all used, and because both Jack and his father are male. But let's look at it another way.

Jack's dad made it clear that Jack's actions were unacceptable, and that Jack would be in serious trouble in the future if he wasn't more responsible.

The second example is almost the same length as the first example, but it's significantly clearer and easier to understand.

ORPHANED DIALOGUE

Orphaned dialogue is a common problem for fiction writers who switch from writing scripts to writing novels, but newer writers also struggle with it because it's largely a problem of formatting.

If you've already read my *How to Write Dialogue: A Busy Writer's Guide*, then you'll remember that, every time you have a new speaker, you need a new paragraph, even if the dialogue is only one word long.

I hope you'll also recall that I recommended you usually place your beat (the action) before your dialogue or at the first natural pause in the dialogue. If you choose to break this rule, I advised you to make sure you had a good reason for it.

These aren't arbitrary guidelines. They're recommended because they make your writing flow better and sound more natural, but also because they help you avoid orphaned dialogue. I'll walk you through the different ways dialogue can become orphaned, and you'll quickly be able to see in some of the examples how following these guidelines could have avoided the problem.

Orphaned dialogue usually happens because, as writers, we know exactly who's speaking. We forget that the reader can read only our words, not our minds.

Too Many Lines of Unattributed Dialogue

We can have a speaker "claim" their dialogue using either a tag (like *said* or *asked*) or through an action beat.

Action Beat: My brother patted Luna's head. "Your dog looks like an alien."
Tag: "Your dog looks like an alien," my brother said.

However, not every line of dialogue needs a tag or a beat to identify the speaker. If you have only two speakers in a scene, you can leave up to three or four lines unattributed.

> Frank tossed the apple to Mary. "An apple a day and all that."
> "I don't like apples."
> "Everyone likes apples."
> "Not me. They crunch. I don't like fruit that crunches."
> Frank held up a hand. "Give it here, then. No sense letting it go to waste."

Orphaned dialogue can happen when we leave dialogue unattributed for more than three or four lines. Three or four lines is the most people can easily keep track of. Once you go beyond that, you risk the reader needing to count backward through the dialogue to figure out who's speaking. (Three is a guideline, not a rule. Occasionally you can have more, but you need to be very careful that it's not confusing.)

Scenes With Multiple Speakers

Scenes with multiple speakers are especially problematic because we need to be certain it's clear who each line of dialogue belongs to. An unattributed line of dialogue could belong to anyone present. Let me give you an example to show you what this might look like. It will also demonstrate how following the two guidelines of a single speaker per paragraph and placing the beat before the dialogue makes sure we're not leaving our dialogue orphaned.

In this example, we have three characters. Dorene, Dorene's son Edgar, and the nun (Sister Mary Martha) who has come to speak to Dorene about Edgar's behavior in school.

> Dorene sighed and shuffled over to her stove. She fished around in the cupboards above.

"Do you mind if I have a cup of tea while we talk?"
She glanced at Sister Mary Martha.
"Would you like one?"
Sister Mary Martha shook her head. Dorene fumbled with the lid on the kettle.
"I would like one."
Edgar peeked hopefully at Dorene. Dorene scowled.
"I didn't ask you."

It's almost impossible at times to know for sure who's speaking. We can guess, but it's not clear, and as soon as something isn't clear, you risk losing the reader. Here's how it should have been written.

Dorene sighed and shuffled over to her stove. She fished around in the cupboards above. "Do you mind if I have a cup of tea while we talk?" She glanced at Sister Mary Martha. "Would you like one?"

Sister Mary Martha shook her head. Dorene fumbled with the lid on the kettle.

Edgar peeked hopefully at Dorene. "I would like one."

Dorene scowled. "I didn't ask you."

I didn't change any of the wording. All I did to make sure our dialogue wasn't orphaned was follow the guidelines about beats and paragraphing. Now, even though we have multiple characters in this scene, it's absolutely clear who is saying what.

Writing About Two Characters in the Same Paragraph

But the sneakiest of the forms of orphaned dialogue is when we write about two characters in the same paragraph and then tack on a line of dialogue at the end.

Ellen waved her arm above her head, and Frank sprinted toward her. "I've missed you."

Who said "I've missed you"? It could be Frank or it could be Ellen, and the reader has no way to tell which one it really is.

> Ellen waved her arm above her head.
> Frank sprinted toward her. "I've missed you."

Now we know that it's Frank who says "I missed you."

When it comes to avoiding orphaned dialogue, always ask yourself, "If I hadn't written it, would I know who was speaking?

CHAPTER TWENTY-THREE

Take It to the Page: Part Four

Many of the elements in this section are things you'll need to watch for as you read through your book for your final self-editing pass. Unfortunately, there's no real shortcut to catching misplaced modifiers or your characters doing the impossible.

We can, however, search for one poison word: *as*.

Use the Find and Replace feature in your word processing program this time. Here's what you should enter.

Find: as

Replace: AS

(Make sure you put a space in front of and behind "as" or that you select "Whole Words Only" otherwise your search will show you every time an *a* appears next to an *s*.)

By replacing the smaller case *as* with all caps, they'll jump out at you.

For every AS, ask yourself the following questions.

- ✓ Have you reversed cause and effect? If so, make sure you have the action come first, followed by the reaction.
- ✓ Have you created a situation where two things are grammatically happening at the same time that can't actually happen at the same time? Rewrite it as two separate sentences to show the real sequence of events.

For any *as* that serves a legitimate purpose in the sentence, simply change it back to the lowercase.

PART FIVE

"Rules" You Can Safely Ignore When Writing Fiction

CHAPTER TWENTY-FOUR

Grammar Taboos That Aren't

Throughout this book, you might have noticed me using certain grammar conventions that your high school teachers taught were wrong. Well, they still are in formal English (such as scholarly journal articles), but for blog posts, magazine articles, and fiction, you can use all of them freely, without fearing repercussions.

SENTENCE FRAGMENTS

A sentence fragment is a part of a sentence, standing alone. It's incomplete because it lacks a subject, a predicate, or sometimes both. I've underlined the sentence fragments in the example below.

She couldn't. <u>Not here. Not now.</u>

Sentence fragments are part of what add variety to informal writing. For fiction writers, they also make internal dialogue and spoken dialogue feel more realistic. We all use sentence fragments when we talk and when we think.

SPLIT INFINITIVES

An *infinitive* is most easily recognized as *to* tacked on to the front of a verb.

> To forbid
> To oppose
> To run
> To sing

Many high school teachers tell their students not to put anything in between the *to* and its verb.

People have been breaking this "rule" since the 1300s, and there's nothing wrong with doing so if it's the best way to write the sentence.

After all, who's going to argue that *to boldly go* should have been *to go boldly*?

BEGINNING A SENTENCE WITH A CONJUNCTION

This is the same type of situation as the sentence fragment above. You don't want to begin a sentence with a conjunction (e.g., *and, but*) in formal writing, but for blog posts, magazine articles, non-fiction books, and novels, go for it.

> I knew I should go to the dinner. But I didn't want to.

The caveat is that you don't want to overdo it, and you should make sure you're using it for the sake of emphasis or cadence rather than just because you can.

ENDING A SENTENCE WITH A PREPOSITION

A *preposition* is a positioning word (e.g., *at, by, for, into, off, over, under, up, with*).

The problem with saying you shouldn't end a sentence with a preposition is that a perfectly good sentence like...

Find out where he came from.

turns into the awkward...

Find out from where he came.

Feel free to ignore anyone who tells you that you can't end a sentence with a preposition, and only abide by this rule if you're writing historical dialogue or a pretentious character.

ANYTHING GOES IN DIALOGUE...ALMOST

Earlier in this book, we talked about punctuation rules and how to properly format your dialogue. Those always apply.

But when it comes to grammar, misused or confused words, and almost everything else, you can throw it out the window when you're writing dialogue as long as you're true to your character in doing so. Even the most grammar-conscious among us don't abide by all the rules when they speak.

Do the Grammar Checks Provided by Word Processing Programs Work?

Grammar and spelling checks provided by word processing programs are great at helping you catch issues in your work, such as spelling mistakes, grammar errors, or using passive voice instead of active voice. But trusting them unquestioningly is dangerous. Extremely dangerous.

For example, in my work as an editor, it's not uncommon for Word to underline a phrase it thinks is grammatically incorrect. I right-click the word/phrase to see Word's suggested change, make that change, and then frown when Word underlines the word/phrase I just changed and suggests that I change it back. Needless to say, the never-ending circle of changes like that causes me a massive headache.

The grammar checks in word processing programs can be helpful, but they're far from perfect. Not only do they sometimes mark a sentence as incorrect no matter what you do to it, they also occasionally mark something as incorrect when it's correct because they're not smart enough to know the difference. They work on a set of hard rules when English grammar is actually rather fluid depending on the specific situation.

For example, some phrases or word orders also get marked as being grammatically incorrect when they are actually correct.

Do you remember when we talked about commonly confused words? The grammar and spelling check in your word processing program will often miss those. After all, the spelling is correct for some words...it's just not the word you meant.

Finally, word processing programs aren't always great at dealing with spelling. For example, words with a *z* in them are almost always spelled with an *s* in British English, often with an *s* in Australian English, rarely with an *s* in Canadian English, and never with an *s* in U.S. English. Examples include *realize, theorize, standardize, tenderize,* etc. However, in Australian English, for example, many of those words are spelled correctly with either the *s* or the *z*, while they are almost never used with a *z* in British English.

Word processing programs' dictionaries don't contain every possible word or every possible spelling (even if you specify the correct language). Because of this, they often mark correctly spelled words as being spelled incorrectly.

This issue of spelling due to differences in versions of English also crops up in the *which/that* debate, as it is very normal for British and Australian English to use *which* to lead off restrictive clauses.

Spelling and grammar checks are invaluable tools, but you should make sure to arm yourself with the grammar knowledge you need in order to know if your word processor is wrong.

200 Commonly Confused Words

T his list is by no means comprehensive. The English language is full of words that sound alike or look alike, but this is a list of the 200 sets that we've most commonly seen confused. It gives you a place to start in building your own personal list.

ail, ale
air, heir
aisle, I'll, isle
allowed, aloud
altar, alter
arc, ark
ate, eight
oar, or, ore
axel, axle
bail, bale

ball, bawl
bare, bear
baron, barren
bazaar, bizarre
beach, beech
bean, been
beat, beet
beau, bow
beer, bier
berth, birth
blew, blue
boarder, border
born, borne
bough, bow
boy, buoy
brake, break
bread, bred
bridal, bridle
broach, brooch
buy, by, bye
cede, seed
ceiling, sealing
cell, sell
cent, scent, sent
cereal, serial
cite, sight, site
coal, kohl
coarse, course
colonel, kernel
complement, compliment
council, counsel

creak, creek

cue, queue

currant, current

cymbol, symbol

dear, deer

descent, dissent

desert, dessert

dew, due

die, dye

discreet, discrete

doe, dough

dose, doze

dual, duel

earn, urn

ewe, yew, you

faint, feint

fair, fare

faun, fawn

faze, phase

feat, feet

fir, fur

flair, flare

flea, flee

flew, flu, flue

flour, flower

for, fore, four

foreword, forward

forth, fourth

foul, fowl

gait, gate

genes, jeans

gild, guild

gilt, guilt

gorilla, guerilla

grate, great

greave, grieve

grisly, grizzly

groan, grown

hail, hale

hair, hare

hall, haul

hangar, hanger

hart, heart

heal, heel, he'll

hear, here

heard, herd

hew, hue

higher, hire

hoard, horde

hoarse, horse

holey, holy, wholly

hour, our

idle, idol

knead, need

knew, new

knight, night

knit, nit

knock, nock

knot, not

know, no

lain, lane

lam, lamb

laps, lapse

leach, leech

leak, leek

lie, lye

loan, lone

lose, loose

mail, male

main, mane

maize, maze

mantel, mantle

marshal, martial

meat, meet

medal, meddle

moor, more

moose, mousse

morning, mourning

muscle, mussel

naval, navel

none, nun

one, won

or, ore, oar

pail, pale

pain, pane

pair, pare, pear

pause, paws

pea, pee

peace, piece

peak, peek, pique

peal, peel

pedal, peddle

peer, pier

plain, plane

plum, plumb

praise, prays, preys

principal, principle

rain, reign, rein

read, reed

real, reel

reek, wreak

rest, wrest

retch, wretch

right, rite, write

ring, wring

road, rode

role, roll

root, route

rose, rows

rung, wrung

rye, wry

spade, spayed

sale, sail

scene, seen

seam, seem

seas, sees, seize

sew, so, sow

shear, sheer

sink, synch

slay, sleigh

sole, soul

some, sum

son, sun

stair, stare

stake, steak

stationary, stationery

steal, steel

straight, strait

sweet, suite

tale, tail

team, teem

tear, tier

there, their, they're

throne, thrown

thyme, time

tic, tick

tide, tied

to, too, two

toad, toed, towed

vain, vane, vein

vial, vile

wail, whale

waist, waste

wait, weight

waive, wave

ware, wear, where

way, weigh, whey

weak, week

weather, whether

wet, whet

which, witch

while, wile

whine, wine

whirl, whorl

whit, wit

woe, whoa
wood, would
your, you're
yoke, yolk

Glossary of Fiction Terms

Because this is a book for fiction writers, we used terms throughout that we expected writers to know and be comfortable with. But if you're a newer writer, you might not have known what all those terms meant. That's where this glossary comes in. We won't cover every fiction writing term, but we will cover (briefly) the terms and concepts we mentioned in this book. If you realize there's something you've never heard of here, please check out the other books in the Busy Writer's Guide series and visit Marcy's website at www.marcykennedy.com.

Backstory – Backstory is everything that happened prior to the first page of your book.

Dialogue – Dialogue is the words your characters speak. Spoken dialogue is always placed between quotation marks in modern fiction (unless you're writing fringe experimental fiction).

Internal Dialogue - The simplest definition is that inner dialogue is what your character is thinking. However, because the definition is so simple, a lot of writers get confused about the difference between the character thinking naturally to themselves and a character narrating for the benefit of the reader. Inner dialogue is not narration.

Flashback – A flashback is when you break the chronological sequence of the story to show something that happened in the past. A flashback can be as short as a sentence or a paragraph or as long as a whole scene or chapter. Flashbacks are used to provide backstory and to give the reader insight into a character's motivation or to provide context for what's currently happening in the "present day" of the story. Flashbacks are tricky and should be used with caution if at all because they bring the forward motion of the story to a grinding halt.

Point of View (POV) - When we talk about POV, we basically mean the point of view from which the story is told. Who are you listening to? Whose head are you in? In a practical sense, POV lays the foundation for everything you'll write in your story, and it comes in four types: first-person, second-person, limited third-person, and omniscient.

Third-Person POV (Third-Person Narrator) - In third-person, a scene, chapter, or sometimes even the whole book is told from the perspective of a single character, but it uses *he/she*.

> Melanie dug through her purse. No keys. They were here yesterday. She'd dropped them in when she came home from work, hadn't she? She tipped her purse's contents out onto the table, and receipts, old gum wrappers, and pennies spilled everywhere.

Everything is filtered through the eyes of the viewpoint character, and we hear their voice. You can have multiple third-person POV characters per book as long as you don't hop between them in a single scene.

First-Person POV (First-Person Narrator) - Just like it sounds, in first-person, the character is telling us the story directly using *I/we*.

> *I dug through my purse. No keys. They were here yesterday. I'd dropped them in when I came home from work, didn't I? I tipped my purse's contents out onto the table, and receipts, old gum wrappers, and pennies spilled everywhere.*

Other Books by Marcy Kennedy

For Writers

Mastering Showing and Telling in Your Fiction

You've heard the advice "show, don't tell" until you can't stand to hear it anymore. Yet fiction writers of all levels still seem to struggle with it.

There are three reasons for this. The first is that this isn't an absolute rule. Telling isn't always wrong. The second is that we lack a clear way of understanding the difference between showing and telling. The third is that we're told "show, don't tell," but we're often left without practical ways to know how and when to do that, and how and when not to. So that's what this book is about.

Chapter One defines showing and telling, and explains why showing is normally better.

Chapter Two gives you eight practical ways to find telling that needs to be changed to showing, and guides you in understanding how to make those changes.

Chapter Three explains how telling can function as a useful first-draft tool.

Chapter Four goes in-depth on the seven situations when telling might be a better choice than showing.

Chapter Five provides you with practical editing tips to help you take what you've learned to the pages of your current novel or short story.

Mastering Showing and Telling in Your Fiction: A Busy Writer's Guide also includes three appendices covering how to use *The Emotion Thesaurus*, dissecting an example so you can see the concepts of showing vs. telling in action, and explaining the closely related topic of As-You-Know-Bob Syndrome.

How to Write Dialogue

How do you properly format dialogue? How can you write dialogue unique to each of your characters? Is it okay to start a chapter with dialogue? Writers all agree that great dialogue helps make great fiction, but it's not as easy to write as it looks.

In *How to Write Dialogue: A Busy Writer's Guide*, you'll learn

- how to format your dialogue,
- how to add variety to your dialogue so it's not always "on the nose,"
- when you should use dialogue and when you shouldn't,
- how to convey information through dialogue without falling prey to As-You-Know-Bob Syndrome,
- how to write dialogue unique to each of your characters,
- how to add tension to your dialogue,
- whether it's ever okay to start a chapter with dialogue,
- ways to handle contractions (or a lack thereof) in science fiction, fantasy, and historical fiction,
- tricks for handling dialect,
- and much more!

Each book in the *Busy Writer's Guide* series is intended to give you enough theory so that you can understand why things work and why they don't, but also enough examples to see how that theory looks in practice. In addition, they provide tips and exercises to help you take it to the pages of your own story with an editor's-eye view.

Strong Female Characters (A Mini-Book)

The misconceptions around what writers mean when we talk about strong female characters make them one of the most difficult character types to write well. Do we have to strip away all femininity to make a female character strong? How do we keep a strong female character likeable? If we're writing historical fiction or science fiction or fantasy based on a historical culture, how far can we stray from the historical records when creating our female characters?

In *Strong Female Characters: A Busy Writer's Guide*, you'll learn

- what "strong female characters" means,
- the keys to writing characters who don't match stereotypical male or female qualities,
- how to keep strong female characters likeable, and
- what roles women actually played in history.

How to Write Faster (A Mini-Book)

In *How to Write Faster: A Busy Writer's Guide*, you'll learn eight techniques that can help you double your word count in a way that's sustainable and doesn't sacrifice the quality of your writing in favor of quantity.

In our new digital era, writers are expected to produce multiple books and short stories a year, and to somehow still find time to build a platform through blogging and social media. We end up burning out or sacrificing time with our family and friends to keep up with what's being asked of us.

How to Write Faster provides you with tools and tips to help you find ways to write better and faster, and still have fun doing it, so that you'll have time left to spend on living life away from your computer. This book was written for writers who believe that there's more to life than just the words on the page, and who want to find a better balance between the work they love and living a full life. The best way to do that is to be more productive in the writing time we have.

Fiction

Frozen: Two Suspenseful Short Stories

Twisted sleepwalking.

A frozen goldfish in a plastic bag.

And a woman afraid she's losing her grip on reality.

"A Purple Elephant" is a suspense short story about grief and betrayal.

In "The Replacements," a prodigal returns home to find that her parents have started a new family, one with no room for her. This disturbing suspense short story is about the lengths to which we'll go to feel like we're wanted, and how we don't always see things the way they really are.

ABOUT THE AUTHOR

Marcy Kennedy is a speculative fiction and suspense writer who believes fantasy is more real than you think. It helps us see life in this world in a new way and gives us a safe place to explore problems that might otherwise be too difficult to face. Alongside her own writing, Marcy works as a freelance editor and teaches classes on craft and social media through W.A.N.A. International.

She's also a proud Canadian and the proud wife of a former U.S. Marine; owns five cats, two birds, and a dog who weighs as much as she does; and plays board games and the flute (not at the same time). Sadly, she's also addicted to coffee and jelly beans.

You can find her blogging at www.marcykennedy.com about writing and about the place where real life meets science fiction, fantasy, and myth. To sign up for her new-release mailing list, please visit her website. Not only will you hear about new releases before anyone else, but you'll also receive exclusive discounts and freebies. Your email address will never be shared, and you can unsubscribe at any time.

Contact Marcy
Email: marcykennedy@gmail.com
Website: www.marcykennedy.com
Twitter: @MarcyKennedy
Facebook: www.facebook.com/MarcyKennedyAuthor

Printed in Great Britain
by Amazon